NORSE MYTHOLOGY

THE GODS, GODDESSES, AND HEROES HANDBOOK

From Vikings to Valkyries, an Epic
Who's Who in Old Norse Mythology

KELSEY A. FULLER-SHAFER, PHD
Illustrated by Sara Richard

ADAMS MEDIA
NEW YORK LONDON TORONTO SYDNEY NEW DELHI

Adams Media
An Imprint of Simon & Schuster, Inc.
100 Technology Center Drive
Stoughton, Massachusetts 02072

First Adams Media hardcover edition October 2023

ADAMS MEDIA and colophon are registered trademarks of Simon & Schuster, Inc.

For information about special discounts for bulk purchases, please contact Simon & Schuster Special Sales at 1-866-506-1949 or business@simonandschuster.com.

The Simon & Schuster Speakers Bureau can bring authors to your live event. For more information or to book an event, contact the Simon & Schuster Speakers Bureau at 1-866-248-3049 or visit our website at www.simonspeakers.com.

Interior design by Sylvia McArdle
Illustrations by Sara Richard
Interior images © 123RF

Manufactured in China

10 9 8 7 6 5 4 3 2 1

Library of Congress Cataloging-in-Publication Data has been applied for.

ISBN 978-1-5072-2052-8
ISBN 978-1-5072-2053-5 (ebook)

DEDICATION

With gratitude to a most excellent friend and accomplice, C.M.B.

ᛉᚲᚠᛏᛝᛁ ᛏᚠᛗ ᛗᚲ ᚾᚲ ᚱᚾᛏᚠᚱ ᛉᚲ ᚹᛗᚱ

CONTENTS

4

PART 3

THE JOTUN
AND OTHER VILLAINS... 94

PART 4

HUMAN HEROES . . . 148

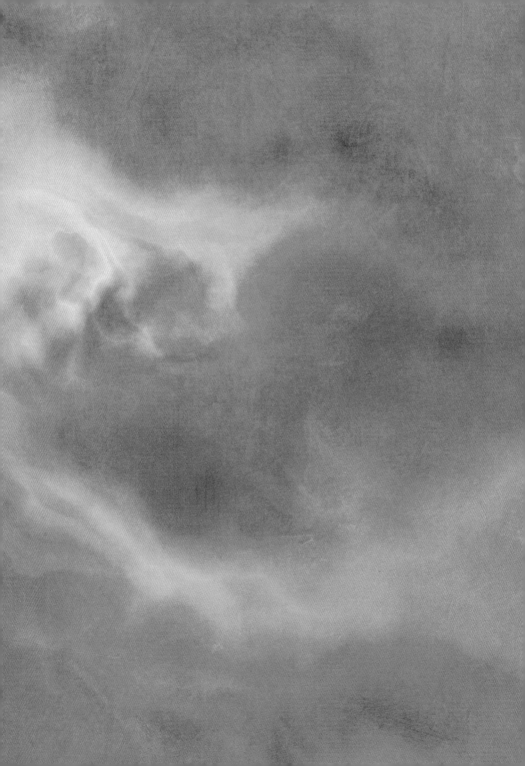

INTRODUCTION

Incredible adventures; stunning heroism; epic battles of sword and wit; and stories with romance, humor, drama, and tragedy: It's no wonder that the world of Norse mythology remains popular today, even though its stories are over a thousand years old. If you want to learn more about the unforgettable characters you've met on movie or TV screens, in video games, or in book pages, *Norse Mythology: The Gods, Goddesses, and Heroes Handbook* is here to introduce you to them in their original domain. You'll discover key characters' names and their English translations, their origin stories, and the most famous adventures they're involved in—plus, you can enjoy dozens of stunning images of these impressive figures.

Norse mythology centers around deities who, much like the humans who deified them, had to contend with strong personalities, challenging environments, and the looming prospect of mortality...in other words, timeless problems! Their trials and tribulations give us a window into the values and customs of the Viking era—such as its focus on loyalty, beauty, and wisdom. In this book, you'll learn how those values shaped dozens of Norse mythology characters—beloved heroes, brave warriors, and frightening monsters alike.

In order to fully explain the history, background, and tales of this extraordinary mythology, this book is broken down into four parts:

- ≫ **Part 1: What Is Norse Mythology?:** Are you picturing a brawny guy with a horned helmet? A hammer that can only be lifted by one god? Sorry to be the bearer of bad news—you've been misled by a century of pop culture! This part will cover what a "Viking" actually was, and how we know what we know (and don't know!) about Norse mythology. It will also summarize the basic story arcs and explain how the individual characters fit into them.

- ≫ **Part 2: The Aesir and Vanir:** Here, you'll meet the gods and goddesses of the Norse pantheon. This part outlines character profiles, Old Norse name translations, and the stories about each of them, as well as alternate spellings to help you keep track of who is who across different translations of the main texts.

- ≫ **Part 3: The Jotun and Other Villains:** Here, you'll explore the antagonists in the myths, including the Jotun (giants!) and other supernatural creatures, and their many conflicts with the gods.

- ≫ **Part 4: Human Heroes:** The term "hero" here will be used…loosely. Many human characters achieved remarkable feats like slaying dragons, uniting kingdoms, and interacting with gods, and yet they also sometimes commited horrible mistakes and met tragic ends.

Whether you want to brush up on your Old Norse trivia (where do the names of our weekdays come from?); better understand a piece of pop culture (such as the *God of War: Ragnarök* video game or *Vikings* TV show); discover the centuries-old origins of characters that appear in your favorite comic books, movies, and TV shows; or just enjoy these exciting stories, *Norse Mythology: The Gods, Goddesses, and Heroes Handbook* gives you a front row seat for the classic tales of these larger-than-life icons.

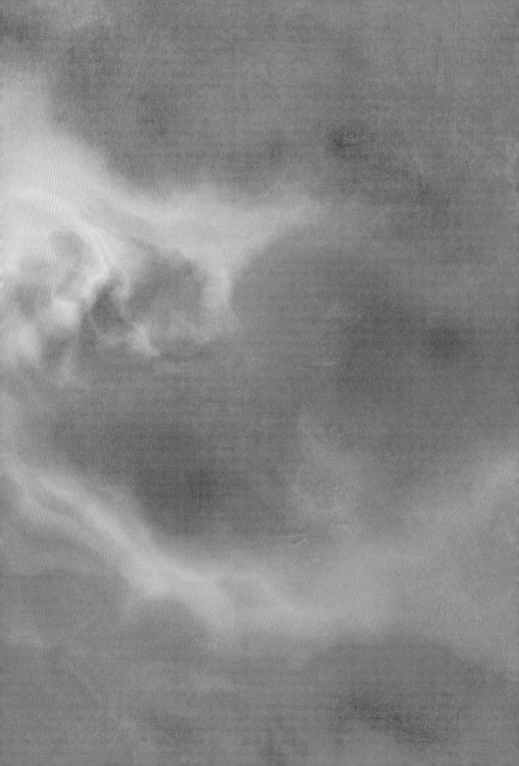

PART 1

WHAT IS NORSE MYTHOLOGY?

B efore you learn about specific characters, it helps to understand the history and overarching storylines of Norse mythology. In this part, you will meet the premedieval Scandinavians who told these stories. They aren't always as they appear in our popular culture of today, and the truth isn't always stranger than fiction. Then, you'll discover key primary source texts that held these stories: where and when they were written, and by whom—and why they matter.

Finally, we'll introduce the foundations for the stories themselves. Most stories are episodic or loosely connected adventures, but there are a few important events that form a cohesive narrative, with the mythological timeline having a clear beginning and end. So, before you meet the individual characters and the stories that define them, we'll take a step back and look at the big picture: the creation of the universe; the world tree Yggdrasil as the setting for the mythology; and the destruction myth, called Ragnarok. These concepts will help all the individual episodes make more sense.

WHO WERE THE VIKINGS?

The Viking age (roughly 793–1066) captures the imagination with tales of adventure and conquest. However, most of the people who lived in the Nordic region during this era were not, in fact, Vikings. There could have been as many as a million people (or Norsemen, if you prefer) living in Norway, Sweden, and Denmark during the Viking age, and isn't Europe lucky they weren't *all* menaces? The word "Viking" specifically describes a person on a boat raiding abroad, so the closest synonym would be "pirate." Plenty of Nordic people lived simpler lives as farmers, merchants, or poets—but a few of them would also work seasonally as Vikings to collect summer bonuses when the weather was fair.

Maybe that's why, today, we picture Vikings as shaggy barbarians who roamed the seas, leaving behind a wake of death and destruction. While yes, there definitely was some pillaging and burning, there was a lot of building too. Several modern-day Scandinavian cities are built on the shoulders of Viking-era towns, and Norsemen were the first founders of cities like Dublin, Ireland, and Kyiv, Ukraine. They explored vast territories from Greenland to Istanbul, both peacefully traded with and terrorized most of Europe, and built settlements throughout the Scottish Isles and beyond. Both destruction and construction remain integral parts of the Viking legacy.

When Was the Viking Age?

The Viking age lasted about three hundred years. In the year 793, Vikings destroyed Lindisfarne Abbey in the Anglo-Saxon territory of Northumbria (England), and word quickly spread about those hostile, heathen raiders from the north. This event typically marks the beginning of the Viking era. The era ended about the time of the Norman Conquest in 1066. That year, the Norwegian king Harald Hardrada tried to conquer England but was defeated by the Duke of Normandy, William the Conqueror. After that, the reputation of the Vikings dwindled and their lifestyle changed: less piracy, more settling down.

Viking Customs and Values

Many of Viking society's values are reflected in its mythology. For example, here are some of its key tenets, which you will see in various forms within the mythological stories:

- They lived by the Norse code of honor: Stand by your family, and face your enemies with courage, even if that means murder and robbery.
- They believed in fate over free will.
- They believed an ideal man kept his word and didn't boast without follow-through. He was also fearless and brave in the face of conflict, and he avoided shame by defending the reputation of himself and his family.
- Though Norse women had some rights not available to women elsewhere (such as divorce under certain circumstances), this was very much a male-dominated society.
- Only free men were allowed to participate in government, and structures like slavery, misogyny, and other forms of discrimination were common practices.
- Vikings were vain, and both attractiveness and unattractiveness were commented on in rather blunt terms. Women were often described as being so beautiful that they radiated light or flat-out called ugly. As for the men,

those shaggy barbarians in the horned helmets? Far from reality. The horned helmets were an invention of the nineteenth century, popularized by artists, illustrators, and costume designers for operas and stage plays. And archaeologists often find combs included in soldiers' burial sites along with their weapons, suggesting that personal grooming was an important daily ritual and would continue in the afterlife. Attractiveness was also linked to class and could to some extent be used to illustrate or determine your level of privilege in the social hierarchy.

The Rise of Christianity

Though the Norman Conquest in 1066 is generally considered the end of the Viking era, other factors played a role in how the mythology faded from popular belief. For example, even though Christianity came slower to the Nordic region than it did to other parts of Europe, it eventually replaced the pagan practices as the dominant religion from about 975–1020 (depending on the country). So why would Christianity, the later religion, have a major effect on the earlier Norse pagan religion that inspired these myths? It's not about time travel, but rather literacy and who penned the earliest written sources. While snippets, illustrations, and references to the Norse myths exist from the Viking era, the myths themselves were not fully collected and written down until the Viking age had ended, and the gods that appear in the myths were no longer worshipped by the vast majority of Nordic society.

THE POETIC EDDA, THE PROSE EDDA, AND OTHER PRIMARY SOURCES

Where can we read the stories of Norse mythology? There are a few major documents, but here's the catch: They were written down a couple centuries after the pre-Christian beliefs had fallen out of practice. Christianity revolutionized Scandinavia around 975–1020, and our earliest surviving primary sources of Norse mythology weren't written down until the 1200s. Furthermore, they were written in Iceland (which officially converted to Christianity in the year 1000), not the mainland. Sure, two hundred years may not seem like much in the grand scheme of things, but this means that Christianity influenced how and why these stories were written: for entertainment or historical record, not religious purposes. The Christian authors—maybe we should call them editors—changed some things from the way these stories were originally told by their ancestors. We can try to guess what was omitted, adjusted, embellished, or watered down, but to some extent we're playing a game of telephone across a thousand years.

The next problem? Translation. When translating poetry, there's *a lot* of room for interpretation, so not all Old Norse scholars arrive at the same meanings from the texts. Sometimes it's trivial (did they mean black or blue?), but other times key elements of the stories can be tricky to figure out, and a translator will have to make an executive decision that might contradict the decisions of their peers. Many translators have rendered the texts in English, but their efforts vary greatly: Some privilege poetic structure, others accentuate antiquated style, while others prioritize clarity. Since I'm a teacher, I usually go for clarity for students unfamiliar with the texts. If you want to read along, I'll note which translations I'm referencing so we're on the same page and using the same set of educated guesses with regards to the tricky spots.

- **The Poetic Edda or Elder Edda:** Contained in an Icelandic manuscript named the Codex Regius, written in 1270 but cobbled together from an earlier oral tradition (and maybe even long-lost written sources) that was originally composed between 900 and 1150 judging from linguistic characteristics. As the name suggests, the myths are told in the form of poetic verses, with about thirty individual poems represented. I use Jackson Crawford's translation, *The Poetic Edda: Stories of the Norse Gods and Heroes*, copyright © 2015 by Hackett Publishing Company.

- **The Prose Edda or Younger Edda:** Written by Icelandic author Snorri Sturluson (1179–1241) around 1220. The Prose Edda is Snorri's attempt at making a coherent story from the poems, and it smooths over the many inconsistencies in his source materials. I use Anthony Faulkes's translation, *Edda*, copyright © 1987 by Everyman.

- ***The Saga of the Volsungs* (and other legendary sagas):** These sagas tell the history of legendary families for generations, recording and celebrating the (much embellished!) history of heroes and their ancestors, and illustrating several interactions between humans and gods. I use Jackson Crawford's translations, *The Saga of the Volsungs*, copyright © 2017, and *Two Sagas of Mythical Heroes*, copyright © 2021, by Hackett Publishing Company.

- **Heimskringla, or The Lives of the Norse Kings:** Another work by Snorri Sturluson, written around 1230, this is a historical document that mixes in some mythology. I use Erling Monsen and A.H. Smith's translation, copyright © 1990 by Dover.

- **The History of the Danes (or the Latin, if you prefer: Gesta Danorum):** Written by Saxo Grammaticus (c. 1150–1220), who attempted a complete history of Denmark, incorporating several Norse gods alongside historical figures, with considerable artistic license. I use Oliver Elton's translation, copyright © 2006 by Project Gutenberg.

These texts piece together a mosaic that shows today's readers the richness of Viking era mythology and gives us a window into the stories that were told from one generation to the next in earlier centuries as religious parables, as folklore, and as entertainment.

THE CREATION MYTH

The most logical Norse myth to learn first is their explanation of how the world came to be. The Norse creation myth appears in the poem *Voluspa* of the Poetic Edda, as well as in *Gylfaginning* in Snorri's Prose Edda. It goes something like this:

In the beginning, there was nothing but a mighty void called Ginnungagap. Two worlds appeared: Niflheim, an icy world, and Muspell, a burning world of fire. From Niflheim's glaciers, rivers began to flow that would reharden into ice and create a surface in Ginnungagap, but when the hot winds from Muspell melted the ice, a giant named Ymir emerged. From Ymir's sweat as he slept grew a man and woman under his left arm, and his legs reproduced together and birthed yet another son, from whom the Jotun (Norse villains) would descend.

The next creature to emerge from the melting ice was a cow named Audhumla. Audhumla's milk fed Ymir, but what would the cow eat? She licked the salt in the ice, and eventually she licked free another creature: a strong, handsome man named Buri. Buri had a son named Bor who married a Jotun named Bestla, and together they had three sons, the first Aesir gods who would shape the earth: Odin, Vili, and Ve.

These three brothers killed Ymir and dragged his body out into Ginnungagap. From his body and flesh, they made the earth. They spilled his blood and made the sea. The mountains were made from his teeth and bones, and trees from his hair. They made Ymir's skull the sky and his brains the clouds. To protect this earth, now called "Midgard," the brothers used Ymir's eyelashes to build fortifications that would keep the Jotun out. Dwarves emerged out of the rot (possibly the maggots) on Ymir's corpse, and Odin and his brothers arranged and guided the paths of the sun and moon so that they could tell time. As they walked in this new world, the sons of Bor found some logs and from them carved the first human man and woman, named Ask and Embla. They gave them gifts—faces, souls, breath, and voices—and Midgard was to be their home.

Eddic poetry often uses devices called "kennings": words that substitute for other words in the form of allusions, descriptions, or cultural references. Kennings are commonly used for names of gods and other characters, but also for geographical features. For example, the ocean might be called "Ymir's blood," and Yggdrasil might be called "the pole of the earth." In addition to recounting the myths, Snorri also includes a key in the *Skaldskaparmal* section of the Prose Edda to help readers decipher many common kennings used in the Poetic Edda and other earlier texts.

YGGDRASIL, THE LIFE TREE

The creation of Midgard, the land of the humans, accounts for just one realm in the universe of Norse mythology. From a tiny seed floating in the void sprung Yggdrasil, the life tree, which grows around, anchors, and connects nine realms in various ways.

Yggdrasil's Roots

The Eddas tell us that there are nine realms throughout Yggdrasil, though how they are arranged is inconsistent among the sources. In *Gylfaginning* in the Prose Edda, Snorri tells us that the roots reach out in three directions:

1. First, the roots go to Asgard, where gods and goddesses live. Valhalla, Odin's afterlife for warriors killed in battle, is likely conjoined with Asgard, as it's not mentioned as a separate realm.
2. Second, the roots reach to Jotunheim, the realm of the Jotun villains. The path to Jotunheim is tricky: Sometimes the characters walk or ride, sometimes they fly, and sometimes they must cross supernatural barriers. Modern-day scholar Ármann Jakobsson surveyed the Eddas to determine where exactly the Jotun live, and it turns out, they're everywhere! They attack from all directions and live in all sorts of environments, perhaps making Jotunheim a land of utter chaos, both socially and geographically.
3. The third root direction points to Niflheim, the ice world from our creation myth.

However, in the Poetic Edda's poem *Grimnismal,* Odin explains that the three tree roots stretch to:

1. Hel, the underworld for all those who are not warriors who go to Valhalla.
2. Jotunheim (that part is consistent, at least!).
3. Midgard, where humans live. The Aesir built a bridge between Asgard and Midgard called the "Bifrost" so that gods and humans could interact. This is no ordinary bridge, however; if it were easy to cross, the Jotun could use it to invade, so the Aesir constructed the bridge out of fire and rainbow to deter them.

Other realms include Muspell (the fire world), Vanaheim (the original home of the Vanir), Alfheim (land of the elves), and Svartalfheim (land of the "dark elves"—possibly meaning dwarves, where darkness references their habit of living underground).

Yggdrasil's Wells

Yggdrasil has some other geographic features as well. The Well of Mimir, whose waters hold wisdom, is said to be at the roots, and another well called Urd's Well, whose waters are holy and protective, is home to a pair of swans.

Urd's Well is located near the hall of the Norns, three women named Skuld, Urd, and Verthandi. Sometimes they are called sisters, though in the Poetic Edda's *Fafnismal*, it's suggested that the three women are a god, an elf, and a dwarf. Regardless of their species, they are always female, and the Norns weave the fates of all the gods and humans. To prevent Yggdrasil from rotting, they cover the tree with the mud from Urd's Well, which forms a protective coating.

Why must they prevent the tree from rotting? Because of the many creatures that feed off the tree:

- The great serpent Nidhogg and his offspring, who gnaw at the tree's roots.
- Vedrfolnir is called an eagle or hawk interchangeably in the Poetic Edda, but later described by Snorri in the Prose Edda as a hawk that sits on top of an eagle (I guess he didn't want to have to choose between the two). Vedrfolnir lives in the topmost branches of the tree.

Ratatosk the squirrel runs up and down the trunk of the tree, carrying insults between Nidhogg and Vedrfolnir.

 Four stags also live in the branches and eat the leaves.

Conflict Within Yggdrasil

Throughout the realms of Yggdrasil, there is an abundance of violence. The Aesir and Vanir are in constant conflict with the Jotun, and in Midgard, humans are always battling each other. These mythological battlegrounds reflect something of the reality for the people who told these tales: Danger, uncertainty, and the struggle against inevitable mortality are all part of the human experience.

NOW YOU KNOW

The Old Norse word for "fate" and a name of one of the Norns, "Urðr" (anglicized to "Urd") turned into the Old English word "wyrd." By the fifteenth century, the English concept of wyrd (still retaining the meaning "fate") was conflated with "weird" (connoting "supernatural"), and thus the origin of the Weird Sisters. These three witches in Shakespeare's *Macbeth* appear in trinity to pronounce Macbeth's glory and his doom, and they bear a striking similarity to both the Norse Norns and the Fates of Greek mythology.

RAGNAROK, THE DESTRUCTION MYTH

The creation myth and the destruction myth form bookends around the many individual stories and adventures throughout Norse mythology. Just as the creation story is considered important information for the characters to know (they're constantly quizzing each other on "beginning of time" trivia), Ragnarok, or the destruction of the universe, features prominently in their stories too and is described in the Poetic Edda's *Voluspa* and the Prose Edda's *Gylfaginning* as well. Odin in particular is determined to prevent Ragnarok, even though it's inevitable. Many of Odin's actions are motivated by trying to change this sealed fate, and conversely, many of the antagonist Loki's actions encourage the events of Ragnarok. So, what is this impending doom that Odin is desperately fighting?

It all starts with the death of a beloved god named Balder (who also happens to be Odin's son). This instigates a feud between the Aesir and Loki that will eventually break out into a full-fledged war. On one side, Odin, Thor, and the other Aesir will fight on the side of life. Odin will summon his army of the dead to fight against Loki's army of Jotun, who fight on the side of destroying everything. The Jotun ride into battle on a great ship called *Naglfar*, made from the fingernail clippings of the dead. Fenrir, the vicious wolf, and the Midgard Serpent with poisonous venom fight alongside the Jotun.

These two sides battle until there are few left on either side. Odin will be swallowed by Fenrir, and Odin's son Vidar will avenge him and kill Fenrir. Thor will slay the Midgard Serpent but collapse dead from exhaustion after nine more steps. Loki and the Aesir Heimdall will kill each other in combat, as will the Aesir Tyr and Garm, the monstrous guard dog of Hel. Another god, Frey, will be killed by a Jotun named Surt, who will then fan the flames of Muspell until everything burns. That's a lot of names—but the general gist is that the good guys lose and the universe is mostly destroyed, but they manage to take most of the bad guys down with them.

It's not just the gods who need to be concerned about Ragnarok; humans need to be worried too. According to *Voluspa*, humans are partly responsible for the tragedy rippling through-out the realms. We'll know the world is ending when all bonds of kinship and fellowship fail, men turn on their brothers, and dishonor replaces virtue and truce. The Bifrost will break, wolves will swallow the sun and moon, and the earth will crumble and fall into the sea.

But believe it or not, Ragnarok is not all about doom and gloom. Eventually, the universe will be reborn, and a new cycle will begin. While some gods, like Odin, will never resurrect (hence his personal investment in stopping the unstoppable), the beloved god Balder will someday return, and there is our glim-mer of hope for life renewed.

So there we have it—the full circle of life in Norse mythology. The creation myth sets the stage for the harsh world of conflict we're stepping into, and nothing motivates some of our charac-ters quite like the impending end of the universe. In the next three parts of this book, we'll travel through Asgard, Midgard, and Jotunheim to experience the adventures that happen in between these two events and explore themes of morality, mortality, and unshakable destiny as they were imagined by Viking-era Scandinavians.

PART 2

THE AESIR AND VANIR

The pantheon of gods in Norse mythology comprises two conjoined societies or families: the Aesir and the Vanir. The Aesir are the more powerful gods who live in the realm of Asgard, while the Vanir originally inhabited Vanaheim. Perhaps showing a philosophical hierarchy, the higher-ranking Aesir tend to be associated with attributes of human society, such as war, poetry, wisdom, marriage, and knowledge, which represent strength and structure. The Vanir, on the other hand, are associated with natural elements and fertility, which are more passive and innate. However, members of these two groups interact, with several members of the Vanir coming to live in Asgard (we'll talk about how exactly that happened later!). Some of the gods and goddesses are well-developed characters that appear frequently throughout the mythology, while others are more secondary to the storylines, appearing as helpers, lovers, or general acquaintances who observe but do not alter the events, or appear in only a few episodes rather than being central to the big picture of the mythology.

Unlike the conception of God held in Judeo-Christian belief, the Norse deities are not omnipotent. As we see in the creation and destruction myths, their fates have been set since the unfolding of the universe, and ultimately, most of them are mortal. Many know exactly how they will die, but they cannot change their own destinies—the best they can do is meddle in the affairs of humans. While some of the Aesir helped to shape the world as we know it, they did not create the whole universe, and there is much that they do not know and for which they are not responsible. They are not all-seeing or all-knowing, though they have tools and resources to help them gather information about the vast realms of the universe.

Finally, these Norse deities are not considered unquestionable moral authorities. Though they may possess many respectable traits like wisdom and courage, and may have been worshipped by Viking-era Scandinavians and entreated to for aid with basic survival (like fishing and farming), they are not always amicable, nor do they always demonstrate a belief in the sanctity of life like many other godlike figures do. They often bicker, ignore each other's advice, and make mistakes with dire consequences—but despite all that, more often than not, Aesir and Vanir characters are still the heroes.

ODIN

ALSO KNOWN AS: **ODINN, WODEN**
OLD NORSE TRANSLATION: **"LORD OF FRENZY"**
KEY FAMILY MEMBERS: **WIFE FRIGG; SONS THOR,
BALDER, AND HOD (OR HOTH)**

Odin was the leader of the Aesir. He is associated with war (both victory and death in battle are said to be his doing), poetry, knowledge, wisdom, carrion beasts that feast on the dead (like wolves, crows, and ravens), and gallows. His wife was the goddess Frigg, and he was famously the father of Thor, but Frigg was not Thor's mother. Different sources provide different lists of Odin's children, but they all agree that Odin had several children with several different women. A few of the more commonly attested sons throughout the Poetic and Prose Eddas include:

- Balder and Hod (their mother was Frigg)
- Thor (his mother was a Jotun named Jord)
- Vali (his mother was a Jotun named Rind)
- Vidar (his mother was a Jotun named Grid)

His menagerie included two wolves named Geri and Freki; two ravens named Huginn and Muninn ("Thought" and "Memory"), who traveled through the realms to bring him news from abroad; and Sleipnir, the eight-legged horse.

Odin has hundreds of names throughout Old Norse literature. Some of these names are used as titles that describe his status, such as High One (Hávi), All-father (Aldafaðr), or Lord of the Undead (Draugadróttinn), but others are names he assumed under his numerous disguises, such as Greybeard (Hárbarðr) and Masked One (Grímnir).

A constant meddler in the fates of men, Odin often interacted with humans under false names and in disguise as an old man with a long, grey beard; a dark cloak; a wide hat; and leaning on a wooden staff (he inspired J.R.R. Tolkien's description of Gandalf in *The Hobbit* and The Lord of the Rings, though Gandalf is a bit less morally ambiguous). Odin constantly incited conflict and war among humans because he had something to gain from their death: His Valkyries collected the bravest and strongest of the slain from the battlefields and brought them to the afterlife (known as Valhalla), which was presided over by Odin. Valhalla was a great hall where the dead (now called "einherjar") fought each other for sport and drank mead while waiting for Odin to lead them in the coming war of Ragnarok.

Odin was also on a ceaseless but doomed quest for information to help him prevent Ragnarok, and he frequently consulted characters with knowledge of magic and foresight who might be able to help him alter the events of the future. Odin was a bit of a tragic figure: He knew he could not change fate, yet he never stopped trying.

THE STORY YOU NEED TO KNOW:

Odin appears as a character in most of the poems of the Poetic Edda and many stories throughout the Prose Edda. Following his role in the creation myth, many of Odin's actions in the stories of the gods were motivated by his desire to prevent Ragnarok, and his appearances in the sagas involving humans often had him manipulating their fate to grow his army of the dead. Other stories demonstrated the knowledge and wisdom that he had accumulated on his quest, such as high-stakes riddles and trivia contests. We also find brief references to episodes and moments of personal sacrifice from his past tucked into other stories, which perhaps best illustrate Odin's doomed struggle against Ragnarok.

Voluspa, the first poem in the Poetic Edda, describes Odin's conversation with an undead sorceress called a "Volva" (he was questioning her for—you guessed it—information about Ragnarok). She proved her knowledge by telling him a narrative that few but him would know. In this story within a story, Odin attempted to gain the upper hand on the universe's design by consulting the Well of Mimir, whose waters were said to contain secrets of wisdom. But water from the well did not come free, and Odin sacrificed an eye for a drink. This explains Odin's missing eye and the many names associated with that feature, including One-Eye (Hoárr) and Fire-Eye (Báleygr).

The knowledge from the well was not enough to teach him how to stop the coming of Ragnarok. The poem that immediately follows in the Poetic Edda is *Havamal*, a collection of advice Odin gives the reader, which outlines many aspects of the value systems and behavioral expectations of Norse society. It's full of contradictions. Life in the Viking age was messy, as was Odin's own personal code of morality by most standards (for example, he often betrayed his promises of victory to warriors so that they might die and join his einherjar; he was often unfaithful to his wife; and evidence suggests that not all of his sexual partners consented to the encounters), and so naturally his guiding advice would illustrate some of that ambiguity. But toward the end of *Havamal*, Odin turned his advice to the value of runes, their holiness, and the advantages of reading and interpreting them. He described how he pierced himself with a spear and then hanged himself from the tree Yggdrasil as an act of sacrificing himself to—well—himself (he's the boss god, who else could he sacrifice himself to?), and for nine days and nine nights he fasted, consuming no food or water. There he remained until he looked down and suddenly, falling from his gallows, Odin saw the runes in the tree roots. Armed with an alphabet, Odin was able to expand his wisdom and power, and he started carving runes for different purposes throughout the realms.

If you're surprised to hear relatively tame stories about wishing wells and the alphabet from the god of war, be patient! Odin will appear in other stories throughout this book as he interacts with the other characters, living up to his reputation as an instigator of conflict, a bringer of death, and a heavy drinker of beer and mead.

THOR

ALSO KNOWN AS: **ÞORR**

OLD NORSE TRANSLATION: **"THUNDER"**

KEY FAMILY MEMBERS: **FATHER ODIN; WIFE SIF**

Thor is known, above all, for his strength and fearlessness (and ravenous appetite for food and booze). When you've got an enemy that needs slaying, Thor's your go-to friend. While Odin may have been the leader of the Aesir, Thor was the main defender of both Asgard and Midgard, always ready to fight (and kill) the threatening Jotun. His weapon of choice, the hammer Mjolnir, has been an icon of Norse paganism for nearly a millennium, and he is rarely imagined without it. He also sported an impressive red beard, gloves of iron to better grip Mjolnir, and a magic belt that doubled his strength when wearing it.

Thor was the son of Odin and the Jotun Jord, who was a personification of the earth. During the Viking era, Thor seemed to have quite the cult following among both farmers and soldiers. His wife was named Sif, though we know little about her (other than her hair was made out of real gold forged by the dwarves after Loki cut all her natural hair off just to be mean), and they had children who are occasionally named but not active characters in the stories (for example, Thor is briefly referenced as

the father of Mothi in the Poetic Edda's *Hymiskvitha*, and Snorri describes his stepson Ull, a particularly handsome archer and skier, in *Gylfaginning* of the Prose Edda).

Thor lived in the biggest hall ever built, called "Bilskirnir," though it seems he went out adventuring more often than he enjoyed his extensive home. His chariot was pulled by two goats, Tanngniost (or Tanngnjóstr) and Tanngrisnir, and he took his role as the goat god very seriously. For example, in the poem *Hymiskvitha*, we learn that he enslaved two children as punishment for injuring one of his goats. Loki was his frequent traveling companion, which was actually a good thing, despite Loki's position as either an enigmatic troublemaker or an all-out villain conspiring for destruction. While Thor was exceptionally strong, he wasn't exactly the smartest god in the pantheon (think of the stereotypical lovable but dumb jock), and Loki's cunning came in handy to help solve problems that couldn't be fixed simply by smashing skulls.

THE STORY YOU NEED TO KNOW:

Thor is such an integral character in many of the most exciting stories in the Poetic and Prose Eddas, it's hard to pick just one! So instead, here's a list of Thor's greatest hits—in other words, a few examples of where he will appear alongside other characters throughout the following Aesir, Vanir, and Jotun entries:

> ▶ Thor and his pal Tyr went on an adventure to steal a beer cauldron from Tyr's father, the Jotun Hymir, which included a rather intense fishing trip and some smashed glassware.

- When a Jotun named Thrym stole Mjolnir, Thor would have done anything to get his hammer back—even if it meant he and Loki had to do some cross-dressing in Freyja's clothes.

- While he wasn't very smart, Thor could dish out a witty insult or two when the situation required. Not only was he the only god who could shut Loki up when he got going, he could also hold his own against the slander and taunts of a mysterious ferryman called Greybeard.

- The giant Jotun Skrymir challenged Thor's strength in a series of magical tests, but nothing was as it appeared, and Thor was so focused on proving himself that he didn't notice he was being tricked into failure over and over again. Luckily, it was actually a very, *very* good thing for everyone that Thor was not strong enough to lift Skrymir's cat.

- Thor took on an entire family of Jotun, Geirrod and his daughters Gjalp and Greip, but without Mjolnir, he improvised by finding other flaming, sharp projectiles and magic staffs to blow the roof off.

Thor's reputation as a Jotun-killer definitely precedes him, and he was both feared and respected. He is the god who perhaps best embodies the Old Norse word "drengr." A man who is drengr is tough and dependable, follows through on oaths and threats, avenges insults, and above all is never a coward when it comes to conflict and violence. "Drengr" is like "macho," "badass," and "brute" all wrapped up in one word, and it sums up the masculine ideal of the Viking age.

Loki, on the other hand, was the opposite of drengr: sly, slippery, backhanded, dishonest, and not ashamed of gender-bending. That is part of what makes the Thor-Loki duo so entertaining. Snorri tells us in *Gylfaginning* that they had been using their respective talents in tandem to heckle the Jotun since the earliest construction of Asgard's halls. A Jotun smith offered to build the Aesir their giant fortress in exchange for taking Freyja to be his wife (as well as carrying away the sun and moon). Loki accepted his outrageous offer with a few stipulations, tricking him into building the fortress in one winter with no help. But when it looked like the smith might actually succeed, Loki shape-shifted into a mare to…"distract" the builder's stallion, causing the stallion (in his mating frenzy) to destroy part of the building right before the deadline and forcing the Jotun to forfeit all payment. Thor, who had been off killing trolls, returned just in time to repay this Jotun for his failure…by killing him.

Now You Know

In the Marvel comics and films, Thor is reimagined as the Norse god of thunder—an easy assumption, given his name. However, he is not actually among the gods who are closely associated with weather of any kind. He probably got that name originally as a tribute to his personality: quick to anger and slow to forgive (as in, he doesn't), loud and booming, smashing and cracking, and always ready for a fight.

FRIGG

ALSO KNOWN AS: **FRIGGA, FRIG**

OLD NORSE TRANSLATION: **"BELOVED"**

KEY FAMILY MEMBERS: **HUSBAND ODIN; SON BALDER**

Frigg was the Aesir goddess who is most closely associated with marriage and motherhood, and she presided over a resplendent hall called "Fensalir." Demonstrating the male-dominated tendencies of Norse society, Frigg was known predominantly via her connection to powerful and important men: She was Odin's wife and Balder's mother. In kennings and allusions throughout the poems in the Poetic Edda, Balder's death is referred to as the first sorrow of Frigg, while the eventual demise of Odin at Ragnarok is called her second sorrow.

She is also described as having strong relationships with other women. In *Gylfaginning*, the Prose Edda mentions that she had two handmaidens with two very specific jobs:

1. One was named Fulla, a beautiful virgin who kept track of Frigg's shoes and was trusted with all her secrets.

2. The second was Gna, who traveled through the realms doing Frigg's messaging and bidding, riding on a horse named Hofvarpnir that could gallop across both sea and sky (this is probably where the iconography of Valkyries on flying horses comes from).

In the Poetic Edda, poems like *Lokasenna* mention Frigg's gift of prophecy, telling us that she had insights into many things that were fated to happen; but unlike her husband, she rarely ever spoke of the secrets that she knew.

THE STORY YOU NEED TO KNOW:

The role of Frigg is a passive one in the Eddas and sagas. For example, she advised Odin against challenging the Riddle Weaver, a Jotun with a reputation for being all-knowing, to a riddle and trivia contest in the poem *Vafthruthnismal*—the god did anyway. There was a common trope in the Norse sagas, particularly those about humans, involving a woman saying, "Don't do this, it will end badly!" and a man saying, "I'm going to do this anyway," and then things usually *do* end badly. But lucky for both Odin and Frigg, Odin had a very exclusive secret up his sleeve...the secret he whispered to Balder on his funeral pyre, which the Riddle Weaver could never know. (Odin uses this riddle against Heidrek in Part 4 too!)

But Frigg was not always a contrarian—she supported and encouraged Odin's decision to test King Geirroth's hospitality in *Grimnismal* (the Norse society took hospitality *very* seriously). (You can read more about King Geirroth in his entry in Part 3.) In *The Saga of the Volsungs*, living up to her reputation for maternal instinct and motherhood, Frigg convinced Odin and one of his Valkyries to intervene on her behalf in the lives of a childless couple so that they might conceive a child after years of trying (stay tuned for Volsung's story when we get to the human heroes in Part 4).

The one instance where she took matters into her own hands involved her son Balder, and in this story she, too, like her husband, tried to prevent or divert the events of Ragnarok. Determined to protect him, she went around to every living thing and made them swear oaths not to harm him—with the exception of one tiny mistletoe plant that she deemed too young to be asked to swear an oath (we'll get to the rest of that story in Balder's entry).

However, aside from her assertive efforts to protect her son, in most of the stories she was purely content to give advice and let others do her bidding. So *her* story was mostly her simply sitting pretty and interacting with the other characters in dialogue. Turns out, when you're a drop-dead gorgeous queen, you don't have to do much to earn everyone else's respect and admiration.

NOW YOU KNOW

Thank Frigg it's Friday! In English, we have these first three Aesir to thank for some of the names of our weekdays. The Old Norse and Old English roots of our modern Wednesday, Thursday, and Friday are Wotansdag, Torsdag, and Frigedag, which translate to Odin's Day, Thor's Day, and Frigg's Day.

BALDER

ALSO KNOWN AS: **BALDR, BALDUR**
OLD NORSE TRANSLATION: **"HERO," "PRINCE"**
KEY FAMILY MEMBERS: **FATHER ODIN; MOTHER FRIGG;
BROTHER HOD; HALF-BROTHERS THOR AND VALI**

Balder was the favorite son of Odin and Frigg and lived in a hall called Breithablik. He was said to be so handsome that light radiated from him, and he was loved and adored by all. Yet most of the stories about Balder are not about his adventures or brave deeds in battle, but rather about his untimely death.

THE STORY YOU NEED TO KNOW:

As discussed in Part 1, Balder's death was the event that set Ragnarok in motion. This story begins with a Poetic Edda poem called *Baldrs Draumar*, wherein Balder was troubled by disturbing nightmares, so Odin sought out an undead witch called a "Volva" to tell him the meaning of the dreams. Entwined with the prophecy of Ragnarok, they learned that Balder did indeed foresee his own death. But Balder was so radiant and beloved by the gods that Frigg went around to every living thing and made them swear an oath never to harm him. In her journeys, she came across a mistletoe plant and decided that it was too small and young, or otherwise too innocuous, to be asked to swear any oaths.

Now that Balder was seemingly invincible in addition to gorgeous, a new favorite game of the gods was throwing things at Balder to watch them bounce off. He confidently allowed them to do this, knowing that he would be unharmed. Balder's brother Hod was left out of the fun because he was blind and unable to see to aim his throws. But trickster Loki decided to help him participate. He gave Hod the mistletoe plant—the only living thing never to have sworn an oath not to hurt Balder—and helped Hod take aim. Unfortunately for all involved, the mistletoe plant struck and killed Balder, underscoring the futility of striving against Ragnarok, which simply could not be prevented.

Balder's death led to mourning and grief beyond measure in Asgard. Odin, in his rage over the murder of his favorite son, cheated on his wife with a Jotun woman named Rind—a union that immediately produced a son named Vali, who grew to full manhood in one day. Vali then avenged his half-brother Balder's death by killing his other half-brother Hod. It seems a bit unfair—but not altogether surprising considering the way that Norse society viewed people with disabilities (that is to say, not kindly)—that Hod was punished with death for what was on his part an accident. Hod's only mistake was trusting Loki!

Meanwhile Loki, the real instigator and mastermind of Balder's murder, was punished but not killed—he transformed himself into a salmon and attempted escape, but the Aesir caught up to him. He was bound (with the intestines of his own son Narfi) to a rock below a giant serpent whose mouth dripped a burning, poisonous venom. Loki's wife, Sigyn, held a bowl to catch the poison, but when the bowl was full and she had to empty it before it overflowed, the poison dripped on Loki's face and he recoiled in pain with such force that the earth quaked.

Gylfaginning in the Prose Edda adds to the story of Balder's death with characters and events not described in the Poetic Edda. Upon Balder's death, his wife, Nanna, died from grief, and their two bodies, along with Balder's horse, were placed on a burning funeral pyre, which had been built from Balder's fabulous ship called *Hringhorni*. This story could be the origin of the "Viking funeral" we see in popular culture today, though no flaming arrows were involved.

Resurrection is a common element of Balder's story. The Prose Edda tells us that Balder and Nanna were reunited in Hel (the place), and later another brother named Hermod tried to bargain with Hel (the goddess) to resurrect Balder, because he was Odin's favorite son. In the Poetic Edda's *Voluspa*, we learn that after the events of Ragnarok, the Volva predicted that the world would be reborn following the devastation and Balder (and his brother Hod) would return to the halls of the gods in all his former glory.

Now You Know

A favored son who is troubled by ominous dreams, doomed by an arrogant mistake, dies with a secret, has a funeral in a boat, and whose death signals the start of a rather gloomy and pessimistic chain of events? Sounds a bit like J.R.R. Tolkien's Boromir from The Lord of the Rings! As a Nordic philologist, Tolkien borrowed many names, concepts, and tropes from Old Norse mythology and literature for his own fantasy epic. His more complex references are cleverly disguised, almost like a scavenger hunt of Norse influence throughout Middle-earth.

FREYJA

ALSO KNOWN AS: **FREJA, FREYA, FREYIA**

OLD NORSE TRANSLATION: **"LADY"**

KEY FAMILY MEMBERS: **FATHER NJORD;**

BROTHER FREY; HUSBAND ODR

Freyja is often called the goddess of love and fertility. She was one of the Vanir and was integrated into Aesir society after the fallout of the Aesir-Vanir War, during which she was likely exchanged as a hostage along with her father, Njord, and brother, Frey. Above all, she is known for her beauty, but she has a few other trademarks too. She was the owner of an often-borrowed garment: a cloak or suit made of falcon feathers that allowed the wearer to fly. She was also the rightful owner of an often-stolen necklace called the Brisingamen. Her other preferred method of travel besides flying was a chariot pulled by two cats. She would also occasionally ride her pet boar, Hildisvini.

According to the poem *Grimnismal* in the Poetic Edda, Freyja lived in a hall called "Folkvang," where she welcomed into the afterlife half of the (human) soldiers who were killed in battle, leaving the other half for Odin's Ragnarok-ready army of the dead in Valhalla. Her husband was mentioned only briefly under the name Odr, and he was often absent while Freyja traveled in search of him. If you think Freyja and Odr sound similar to Frigg and Odin, you're not alone. One theory is that these two women's names and characters have a common origin in an older Germanic tradition but eventually split into distinct characters (which could be why these two women were conflated in the *God of War: Ragnarök* video game as Odin's ex-wife who can turn into a falcon). Folkvang was also likely not an altogether separate place from Valhalla, as the afterlife for humans was elsewhere clearly divided into only two options: Valhalla or Hel.

THE STORY YOU NEED TO KNOW:

Freyja is one of the few main goddesses and a popular embodiment of beauty, light, and femininity, and she appears in many of the stories throughout the Poetic and Prose Eddas. Her role is usually the same across these stories: She was recognized as being among the most beautiful of women and was shamelessly coveted by antagonistic Jotun. In their attempts to kidnap or seduce her, shenanigans and conflict ensued. These stories about Freyja use what we might today call the "male gaze," where female characters exist mostly for the gratification and objectification of men, and women are introduced into a plot that is actively controlled by the men around them. To her credit, though, Freyja usually managed to get her way and avoid catastrophe.

Thrymskvitha is a particularly playful example from the Poetic Edda that not only illustrates Freyja's role as a desirable woman but also demonstrates some humor surrounding traditional gender expectations. A Jotun king named Thrym stole and hid Thor's hammer, Mjolnir, and Loki borrowed Freyja's feather suit to fly to Jotunheim to negotiate for its return. Thrym demanded that

Freyja be brought to Jotunheim as his bride if Thor wanted his hammer back, which seemed to Thor a reasonable sacrifice to make for the return of his beloved hammer. As you might expect, this bargain was significantly less agreeable to the offended and already-married Freyja. Her anger sent tremors throughout Asgard, and she strongly objected to this plan on the grounds that she would be mocked for such scandalous and loose behavior (which was a justified fear, considering how Loki gossiped and shamed her in another poem from the Poetic Edda, *Lokasenna*), not to mention that the Aesir and Vanir were not particularly friendly with most giants to begin with! With the safety and security of Asgard at risk without Thor and Mjolnir to defend it, the trickster Loki came up with a cunning plan to both satisfy Freyja's pride and regain Thor's property. He dressed the reluctant Thor up as a bride, complete with Freyja's recognizable Brisingamen necklace. Loki then dressed himself up as a bridesmaid, and under this wedding veil of disguise, they traveled together to Jotunheim in apparent agreement with Thrym's terms.

Thrym began to suspect that there was more to "Freyja" than met the eye when, at the engagement feast, he witnessed her ravenous appetite and poor table manners. But Loki the bridesmaid assured Thrym this was only because she hadn't been able to eat for eight days, waiting with anticipation for her wedding day. Thrym lifted the veil and tried to kiss his lovely bride-to-be, but was then startled by her fierce and burning eyes. Loki again reassured him, her eyes were simply bloodshot from eight nights of sleeplessness, kept awake by her eagerness to marry him. Since they had fulfilled their end of the bargain, Loki requested that Thor's hammer be delivered to "Freyja," so that they could rightfully return it to Asgard, and Thrym complied. At this point, Thor could stand the humiliation no longer, and as soon as Mjolnir was in reach, he used it to kill Thrym and his family, and injure most of the other guests present at the feast too.

NOW YOU KNOW

Throughout the myths, our pantheon of Aesir and Vanir lived together in an integrated society. However, in the poem *Voluspa*, from the Poetic Edda, and the *Gylfaginning* section of the Prose Edda, we find hints about how that peaceful coexistence might have started: the Aesir-Vanir War. The Aesir and the Vanir fought until they were so tired that they could fight no more, but when neither side was victorious, they agreed to exchange hostages. What started this war? We're not entirely sure, but according to *Voluspa*, it might have been the way a woman named Gullveig was treated by the Aesir. She was speared and burned three times; but after each time she was murdered, she was reincarnated. This is all we hear about Gullveig and her brutal treatment, but she might have been responsible (along with Freyja) for introducing the Aesir to a type of mystical, prophecy-related Vanir magic called "seidh" ("seiðr"), commonly associated with women (like Freyja, the Volva, and the Norns).

NJORD

ALSO KNOWN AS: **NJORTH, NJORÐR, NIORD**
OLD NORSE TRANSLATION: **POSSIBLY "STRENGTH," "POWER"**
KEY FAMILY MEMBERS: **CHILDREN FREYJA AND FREY; WIFE SKADI**

Njord was worshipped by the Norse as a fertility god, and he is broadly associated with the sea, wind, agriculture, and wealth. He was the father of Freyja and Frey (the identity of their mother is questionable, but she was described in the Poetic Edda poem *Lokasenna* as being both Njord's sister and his wife) and was exchanged as a hostage during the Aesir-Vanir War along with his children.

He lived in a hall called "Noatun," which lay on a coast. The importance of seafaring to Viking-era Scandinavia is evident in the number of cults, place names, and iconography in archaeological remains reflecting Njord. Though his role in the stories is less central than other gods like Odin and Thor, Snorri's *Heimskringla* tells of people making many sacrifices to Njord so that he might support their well-being as well as great sorrow and weeping upon his eventual death. However, in the poem *Vafthruthnismal* in the Poetic Edda, Njord is listed as one of the survivors of Ragnarok, and following the death and destruction of most of the Aesir, it states that he will return to his original home in Vanaheim.

THE STORY YOU NEED TO KNOW:

While we don't know much about Njord's sister-wife and the mother of Freya and Frey, we do have a story in *Skaldskaparmal* in the Prose Edda that describes Njord's rather unhappy marriage to a woman named Skadi (or Skathi), who was the daughter of a Jotun named Thiassi (and therefore not Njord's sister-wife, as he was definitely of the Vanir and not Jotun; so Skadi could perhaps be a remarriage for Njord and stepmother to the twins). Through-out the Eddas, Jotun women are described as being both tempt-ingly beautiful and frustratingly disagreeable, and the story of Njord and Skadi demonstrates both of those attributes in a tale of a rather incompatible relationship.

This story begins with the killing of Skadi's father, the Jotun named Thiassi (or Thjazi), to avenge the kidnapping of the god-dess Ithunn after she was rescued and returned to Asgard (you'll learn about that story when we talk about Ithunn!). Skadi then traveled to Asgard armed and ready for revenge, but instead of fighting her in battle, the Aesir decided they would offer her three different compensations for killing her dad: First, she could choose a husband for herself but must do so by looking at the feet of the eligible bachelors without seeing any other parts of them. She picked the cleanest and best-looking feet, assuming they belonged to Balder, who would be the ideal attractive husband, but those handsome feet in fact belonged to Njord. And so, Skadi and Njord were engaged to be married, and they continued with her other reconciliation prizes.

Her second compensation was that the Aesir had to find a way to make her laugh, a seemingly impossible task—but it was accomplished by the scoundrel Loki, not her new fiancé, Njord. While there were probably safer ways to make a woman laugh, Loki did not take any chances and went for gold on his first try. He took a rope and tied one end to a goat's beard and the other end to his own testicles, and the two proceeded to have a raucous tug-of-war. Whether it was genuine laughter, appalled laughter, or nervous laughter, we'll never know—but laugh she did. And finally, Odin took her father's eyes and threw them into the sky, turning them into stars.

And so Skadi was compensated for the loss of her father, and Njord and Skadi were married. But they immediately began to argue about where they would live. Skadi wanted to ski and hunt in the mountains of Thrymheim, where she was raised and had lived with her father, and she couldn't stand the constant sound of squawking seagulls in Noatun. However, Njord longed to live by the sea, and he told her that the howling of the wolves sounded too harsh to him compared to the songs of the swans that he was accustomed to. They tried to compromise and agreed to alternate, living for nine nights in Thrymheim and then the next nine nights in Noatun. But both parties found this compromise difficult to maintain, and eventually, Skadi left Njord and returned to her mountain home, while he remained in his hall by the sea. In *Ynglinga Saga* from *Heimskringla*, Snorri tells us that after leaving Njord, Skadi ran off to have an abundance of sons with Odin, one of whom was named Saeming, from whom would descend some of the lineages of Swedish kings.

FREY

ALSO KNOWN AS: **FREYR**
OLD NORSE TRANSLATION: **"LORD"**
KEY FAMILY MEMBERS: **FATHER NJORD;
SISTER FREYJA; WIFE GERD**

Like his sister and father, the Vanir Frey is also considered a god of fertility and is associated with sun and rain. His chariot was pulled by a boar named Gullinbursti, and his domain was Alfheim, the land of the elves, which was given to him by the gods as a toothing gift (baby's first tooth? Let's give him a whole realm!). And yet also like his father and sister, Frey was well-liked and respected in Aesir society and considered handsome, honorable, and powerful.

THE STORY YOU NEED TO KNOW:

Frey's main story in the Poetic Edda is *For Skirnis.* It begins with Frey sitting on Odin's throne (called "Hlithskjalf" or "Hlidskjalf") a vantage point from which he could see into all the nine realms. He caught a glimpse of a beautiful woman walking in Jotunheim: Gerd (or Gerth), daughter of Gymir. He was lovesick and infatuated with this beautiful Jotun, and he moped and brooded until Njord and Skadi demanded that Frey's servant, Skirnir, intervene

and find out what could possibly be the matter with Frey. Skirnir was reluctant to do so, not wanting to be on the receiving end of Frey's anger, but he did so anyway. Skirnir assured Frey that, having grown up together and been good friends since childhood, they could trust each other with their troubles.

Frey then described for Skirnir the beautiful, radiant woman he saw in Gymir's garden and determined that no other woman could ever compare to her. The problem, however, was that likely no one would take kindly to the idea of a marriage between himself and this Jotun. Nevertheless, Skirnir decided that he would go to Jotunheim and fetch this woman, but he needed some help to do so. The road to Jotunheim was dangerous, so he asked Frey to provide a horse capable of riding through darkness and fire as well as Frey's magic sword, which would fight enemies on its own. Frey did so without hesitation (even though the loss of his magic sword was perceived to be his doom during Ragnarok, as without it he would be slain), as nothing was worth more to him than having this beautiful woman for a wife.

Braving the fierce dogs guarding her door, Skirnir came to the home of Gerd and pronounced the marriage proposal on Frey's behalf, first offering her eleven golden apples in exchange for her love. Gerd refused, saying for no man, not even for Frey, would she accept eleven apples as a marriage price. He then offered to give her Odin's magic gold ring (the reader is not sure if Odin is aware of this!), which produced eight more golden rings every nine nights, but Gerd assured him that her father was wealthy enough and she had no shortage of gold in her home in Jotunheim.

Realizing that he was getting nowhere with gifts and promises, Skirnir then tried a different approach: threats and curses.
He first threatened to cut her head off, but she told him neither
she nor her father would tolerate this. Skirnir did not take no
for an answer and continued to say that unless she agreed to be
Frey's wife, he would kill her father and beat her until she agreed
to go with him or else hide her in an eagle's nest far away. There,
she would be repulsed by food and starve and see nothing of
the world, only Hel, where she would be forced to drink goat
urine. He cursed her to experience nothing in life but pain, sorrow, and various forms of torture and sexual abuse at the hands
of monsters, trolls, and three-headed giants, never to find love
and instead earn the hatred and rage of Odin, Thor, and Frey.
After she heard this string of curses, Gerd finally agreed that she
would, after nine days' time, meet Frey in a forest grove called
Barri, where they would consummate the marriage.

This poem is downright abusive when taken at face value.
However, it has also been interpreted as an allegory for the coming of spring after winter: Skirnir (the sun) thawed Gerd (the
earth) for fertilization by Frey (agriculture). From that perspec-
tive, the story is fulfilling the role of mythology to explain why
things exist as they do, rather than simply a narrative of sexual
assault for the sake of entertainment.

Now You Know

An eleventh-century church scholar named Adam of Bremen was an early ethnographer of the Germanic lands and Scandinavia. Claiming to have witnessed the pagan practices of a temple at Uppsala, Sweden, in his Latin work, *Gesta Hammaburgensis ecclesiae pontificum* (*The History of the Archbishops of Hamberg-Bremen*), he described seeing statues of Thor, Odin, and Frey. It is from his account that Frey received a reputation for having an *enormous* phallus. Because Adam was a Christian and might have misunderstood or even intentionally exaggerated his accounts of pagan practices, we aren't confident in all his descriptions, but that hasn't stopped people from imagining Frey as an especially well-endowed and erect fertility god. (The Danish historian Saxo Grammaticus also mentioned frequent sacrifices to Frey in his *The History of the Danes*, but includes no additional commentary on his anatomy.)

THE VALKYRIES

ALSO KNOWN AS: **VALKYRJUR (PLURAL), VALKYRJA (SINGULAR)**
OLD NORSE TRANSLATION: **"CHOOSERS OF THE SLAIN"**

The Valkyries were Odin's elite company of shield-maidens, female warriors who often performed a defensive role in warfare, protecting and aiding Odin's chosen human heroes. The Valkyries had two main tasks to fulfill. The first was to do Odin's bidding on the battlefield, interfering in the fates of men by giving supernatural advantage or disadvantage to those favored or fallen in the eyes of Odin. Their second job was to carry the souls of half of the best and bravest warriors slain on the battlefield to the afterlife in Valhalla (Freyja carried away the other half). There, these soldiers became known as the einherjar, Odin's army of the dead, which would rise up to fight for him at Ragnarok. The more einherjar to fight in his hopeless cause, the better—so Odin and his Valkyries had to stir up trouble to make sure there were plenty of courageous and glorious deaths among the humans. The einherjar lived in a warrior's paradise in Valhalla, and the Valkyries brought them mead and beer while they waited for their ultimate battle. The Valkyries were usually of noble origin, either daughters of gods or kings, and they often became the lovers or wives of human heroes.

THE STORY YOU NEED TO KNOW:

In the Poetic Edda, *Sigrdrifumal* describes the human hero Sigurd's encounter with a Valkyrie named Sigrdrifa ("Victory Driver"). This story bears a striking resemblance to other versions of Sigurd's story and his meeting with a Valkyrie named Brynhild, and the two women might even be the same character (you can compare the two in Brynhild's entry in Part 4).

Sigurd was riding off to his next adventure after slaying a dragon and taking its treasure (see the Sigurd entry in Part 4 for more on that tale) when he saw a fortress in the mountains, glowing as if illuminated by fire. Upon arriving, he saw a person dressed in full armor sleeping on the floor. He removed their helmet and noticed this sleeping soldier was a woman, and her chain mail was so tight that it had nearly grown into her skin. So, he took his magic sword, called Gram, and cut her armor off her chest and arms and removed it (this part is a little reminiscent of the later folktale "Sleeping Beauty," and the various other literary iterations of nonconsensual advances on sleeping women).

Removing her chain mail broke the spell and she awakened, asking to know who had freed her from the armor that had imprisoned her in sleep. Sigurd identified himself as Sigmund's son and a worthy warrior, and Sigrdrifa brought him a drinking horn of mead—a ritual expected of the Valkyrie—and described to him the circumstances surrounding how he had come to find her thus. Odin had promised victory in battle to a king and seasoned warrior named Hjalm-Gunnar, but Sigrdrifa used her position as a Valkyrie to defy Odin and kill Hjalm-Gunnar so that his opponent

Agnar might gain the upper hand. As revenge for this disobedience, Odin punished her twice so that she might never rebel or influence the victories of war again: First, he told her that she must marry, though she had already sworn an oath not to marry anyone except a man who had no fear; and second, he pricked her with a sleeping thorn so that she could not wake of her own accord.

Sigurd asked the Valkyrie to teach him wisdom, and her answers demonstrated how deeply connected the Valkyries were to Odin. Much of what she imparted echoed Odin's wisdom in *Havamal* in the Poetic Edda, such as the magic of runes and their proper application for aid with victory, voyages, healing, and good judgment. She then asked Sigurd if he would like some more advice, even though his fate was already sealed. Sigurd assured her that he was not a coward who would run from his destiny and would hear whatever else she could tell him. She gave him several warnings:

- To do well by his kin, because dishonoring his family would be the death of him.
- To be honest and keep his oaths and not waste time talking with fools.
- To kill any idiot who slandered him.
- To be wary of witches and sorceresses and not be seduced by pretty women who were strangers (especially if they were someone else's wife!).
- To avoid drinking too much and becoming careless.
- To not believe the relatives of men he had killed.

- To not desecrate dead bodies he came across no matter how they died.
- To avoid evil if possible—because it seemed likely he'd probably die pretty soon since he was such a great warrior who would fight so many great battles.

For the most part, it's all pretty good advice, though she ended abruptly on a bit of a downer.

The Volva

ALSO KNOWN AS: V**O**LVA, VÖLVA
OLD NORSE TRANSLATION: "PROPHETESS"

The Volva were mystical female prophets or undead witches who could be awoken from the sleep of death to give insights into the future. Often, the Volva told only partial or fragmented stories (probably because they didn't actually *enjoy* being woken up), interwoven with vast amounts of trivia to demonstrate the breadth of their knowledge and flex their credentials. The Volva shared information about the creation and destruction of the universe, the many living things within it, their origins and genealogies, and their dirty secrets. The Volva were practitioners of seidh (seiðr), the Old Norse word for "magic" or "sorcery" that almost always originates with women, though it's rumored that Odin himself dabbled without much questioning of his masculinity.

THE STORY YOU NEED TO KNOW:

The Volva are main characters in two poems in the Poetic Edda: *Voluspa* and *Voluspa en skamma*. We have frequently mentioned *Voluspa*, wherein Odin woke the Volva for information about Ragnarok, and she told him of many things she knew: the nature of the universe and how it was built, the fate of the gods at Ragnarok, and the many classes of creatures throughout the realms. But *Voluspa en skamma* has a few key differences. In this version, which was likely composed as a later addition to the Poetic Edda and possibly the combination of two different poems, Freyja awakened the Volva, and the topic of conversation was not primarily Ragnarok, but the genealogy of her human lover named Ottar.

In this version, the Volva also had a name: Hyndla. Freyja awakened her by calling her name and other titles like "lady," "friend," and "sister" and, perhaps a little less polite, "cave dweller." She told Hyndla that they would ride together to Valhalla to meet Odin and make sacrifices to Thor, who would give Hyndla gifts. Hyndla was not tempted. Instead, she accused Freyja of lying about any kind of reward that she would receive and incited her by telling her that Ottar was following her along the road toward the dead.

Now it was Freyja's turn to accuse Hyndla of lying. She said there was no way that this mortal Ottar was following her. Freyja mentioned Ottar's daring adventures, as well as the temples Ottar had built and the faithful sacrifices he had made for her. She then asked the Volva to give her an account of all the best families among the men of Midgard: the lineages of princes, chiefs, and kings. As the Volva answered, she directed her statements to Ottar—which suggested he may indeed have followed Freyja and arrived just in time for the big reveal.

The Volva told Ottar of the ancestors of his father and that his mother was a beautiful priestess of Hlethi, from a lineage of well-born women. Ottar could count among his ancestors the hero Eymund, who killed Sigtrygg, and Almveig, the "best

of all women" (though to be fair, a lot of women are described throughout the texts as being the best), as well as members from all the noblest families of men, including the Skjoldungs, Skilfings, Authlings, and Ynglings. He descended from many honored and accomplished princes, Vikings, warriors, and dragon slayers, like Sigurd and Hrolf. The Volva then discussed the fates of various gods, denoting the divine origins of many high-ranking Scandinavian royal families, whose histories were intentionally blended with myth as they claimed to be descendants of Odin or other Aesir. She talked about the death of Balder, the marriage of Frey and Gerd, and the birth of a few of Loki's children. Hyndla mentioned the coming of another god following Ragnarok and the death of Odin—though she dared not speak their name—but beyond that, the Volva knew very little of the future following the rebirth of the universe.

Freyja then asked Hyndla for one more favor: a memory-drink for Ottar, so that when he and his friend Angantyr were later discussing their family trees, he would remember all that the Volva had told them. But Hyndla became angry, telling them to leave quickly so that she might return to sleep. She said that the conversation was not happening of her own free will (perhaps a magical intervention forced or compelled her to speak, as Freyja was also a known practitioner of seidh), and bid Freyja to go like a "ewe with her ram"—accusing her of being lustful and promiscuous with both Ottar and Odin. Freyja returned the insult, telling Hyndla that she would strike a fire around her so she would never be able to leave like a "ewe with her ram," leaving her alone without companionship. The Volva was not overly concerned by this threat, saying that most living things endure fire and death and that the only drink she had for Ottar was a poisoned beer. Freyja insisted that no harm would come to Ottar, as he was protected by her and the gods.

They left and the Volva was allowed to return to her slumber until the next time a god or goddess came along to wake her and her sisters up and demand answers to their questions or solutions to their problems.

NOW YOU KNOW

Several stanzas of the Poetic Edda poem *Voluspa* are referred to as a "catalog of the dwarves," and it really is just that: several back-to-back stanzas of dwarf names. We don't know much about them, other than they look like humans but are smaller—and the Volva doesn't tell us their stories, what they do, or why they're worth listing (other than the fact that some of them are related to each other). However, in this catalog we might see some familiar names: Durin, Bombur, Nori, Thorin, Fili, Kili...even Gandalf! Long before he knew that his writings on Middle-earth would become so expansive, J.R.R. Tolkien borrowed several of these names for his children's story, *The Hobbit,* which has since become a literary classic.

HEIMDALL

ALSO KNOWN AS: **HEIMDALR, HEIMDALI**

OLD NORSE TRANSLATION: **POSSIBLY "ILLUMINATOR OF THE WORLD"**

Heimdall was the watchman of the gods, tirelessly guarding the Bifrost, the rainbow bridge between Asgard and Midgard, standing at the ready in case any Jotun tried to invade. He watched and waited to blow the great horn, Gjallarhorn, at the first sign of Ragnarok. His home, a hall called "Himinbiorg," was right next to the Asgard side of the Bifrost.

His birth sounds a bit complicated, as he was the son of nine mothers (no mention of a father), though who those nine women were remains inconsistent across sources: Sometimes they were nine Jotun sisters, or in other references, they were the nine daughters of the Jotun Aegir and personifications of the ocean waves. Heimdall is described as white (probably referring to his skin and hair being extraordinarily pale), his teeth were made of gold, and he had excellent hearing and vision. For example, according to Snorri in *Gylfaginning* in the Prose Edda, he could see a hundred leagues in the dark and could hear the grass growing on earth from all the way up on the Bifrost.

As the guardian of Asgard, Heimdall butted heads with the main antagonist, Loki. For example, in the fragments of an early poem called *Husdrapa*, Loki is disguised as a seal to steal Freyja's Brisingamen necklace, and Heimdall also transforms into a seal and fights seal-Loki to recover it. Ultimately, the stakes became higher than jewelry, and Heimdall and Loki would kill each other in battle at Ragnarok. Like Thor, Heimdall was a protector of humans, and he was also considered the father of all the classes of humanity.

THE STORY YOU NEED TO KNOW:

Heimdall's story in the Poetic Edda is called *Rigsthula*, and in it, he travels around seashores and green roads (which are reminiscent of spring and fertility) under the name "Rig" and has some productive sexual encounters with three human couples. This story clearly outlines the class hierarchy, duties, and lifestyles associated with enslaved people, freeborn people, and nobility in Viking-era Scandinavian society.

As he was walking, Rig came upon a small farmhouse with an open door. He entered and saw an older couple with grey hair sitting next to a fire. Their names were Ai and Edda (meaning "great-grandfather" and "great-grandmother"). They fed him the best food they had to offer, which wasn't much: hard bread made of many grains, a bowl of soup, and boiled meat. For the next three nights, when it came time to sleep, Rig lay between them, the man and woman on either side of him, and he gave them…ahem…"counsel."

Nine months later, Edda gave birth to a child. They named him Slave, and he grew up to be ugly but strong. When Slave was older, an equally ugly woman walked into his life: She had a hooked nose, her skin was burned by the sun, and her name was Slavewoman. They made a bed together and had many children whom they loved and taught well, raising them to build, farm, and do all manners of hard and unpleasant work. Their sons had names like "Barn-Cleaner" and "Hunchback," and their daughters had names like "Shorty" and "Fatty." From this family descended all enslaved people.

Rig continued his journey and found another hall with an open door and entered. He saw a man busy with wood carving and his wife busy weaving. Their names were Afi and Amma ("grandfather" and "grandmother")—they were well-groomed and nicely dressed, and their home was furnished. After dinner for three nights, Rig lay between them in bed, one on each side, and he gave this couple some "counseling" too.

Nine months later, Amma gave birth to a child with red hair and keen eyes (indicating he was capable of being educated), and they named him Freeman. He grew up and worked his own farm and built his own house, and eventually, his parents found him a woman to marry named In-Law. She wore a veil to the wedding (showing that they had wealth), and they exchanged rings and then built a home together. They also had many children, and gave their sons names like "Farmer," "Smith," and "Fighter," and their daughters names like "Smart," "Bride," and "Vivacious." From this lineage descended all the families of free farmers, craftsmen, and herdsmen.

Rig walked on and entered a large hall with an open door and found a husband and wife holding hands. They looked into each other's eyes, and they were happy and affectionate. The husband was busy stringing his bow and making arrows. His wife was more beautiful than snow, with fine jewelry and a headdress, and she smoothed the wrinkles out of her blouse and dress. Their names were Fathir and Mothir ("father" and "mother"), and for dinner they served Rig white bread, meat, poultry, and wine at a well-set table with silverware, a tablecloth, and goblets with gems set in them. They had fine conversation together until the day passed and night came. Rig spent three nights with them as well, providing his trademark "counsel" with the husband and wife lying on either side of him.

Nine months later, Mothir gave birth to a child, and she swaddled him in silk and named him Lord. He grew to be strong and smart, with blond hair and bright eyes, and he learned how to fight with sword and spear, ride horses and hunt with dogs, read runes, and conquer lands. Lord ventured far, won famous battles, and became a wealthy estate owner. Messengers came and offered him a bride named Eagle, who was beautiful, gentle, and wise. They were married and loved each other and had many children, giving their sons names like "Noble," "Heir," and "Nobility." But King, the youngest, was special, possessing the strength of eight men and learning the language of birds, and he became interested in runes. Rig taught him the runes, and King eventually learned more than Rig himself knew. When young King grew tired of shooting arrows at birds, he mounted his horse and started killing men in wars with the rich nearby chieftains so that he might claim their inheritances. Thus did Heimdall's encounters with these early humans in Midgard father all the classes of humanity and ordain for them a set of roles and expectations within Norse society.

TYR

ALSO KNOWN AS: **TÝR**

OLD NORSE TRANSLATION: **"GOD"**

KEY FAMILY MEMBERS: **FATHER HYMIR**

Tyr is acclaimed throughout the Poetic and Prose Eddas as being one of the more important and powerful Aesir: He is associated with the sky and war (hence his prominent position in *God of War: Ragnarök*). He is also described by Snorri in the *Gylfaginning* section of the Prose Edda as one of the great warriors among the Norse pantheon, both valiant and clever, though few stories about him survive. But we do know that he was willing to make a serious personal sacrifice to try to keep the wolf Fenrir under control (we'll get to the story about how he lost his hand later) in the hopes that Fenrir would not eat Odin when Ragnarok came. Tyr would be another casualty of Ragnarok, killed in a struggle with Hel's guard dog Garm, who likewise did not survive the encounter. He didn't seem to have a wife or any children (although in *Lokasenna*, Loki makes one ambiguous snide remark about an unnamed wife who is not mentioned or paralleled elsewhere in the primary sources). Because of both his connection to war and the loss of his hand, he's not considered a god who resolved disputes peacefully.

THE STORY YOU NEED TO KNOW:

Hymiskvitha is the only poem in the Poetic Edda wherein Tyr featured as a primary character, and it offers insight into his family and origins, as well as how firmly Tyr's loyalties were rooted to the Aesir instead of his own Jotun father. It's also a rather amusing story, as it demonstrates how far the gods would go to acquire a cherished and valuable substance: beer.

After a hunting trip, the gods enjoyed a meal, but they became thirsty and decided they needed a drink. After performing some rune magic, they learned that there was a Jotun named Aegir who owned massive cauldrons big enough to brew beer for all the Aesir and Vanir to enjoy together. Thor confronted Aegir and demanded that he provide a massive feast with fresh brews for all the gods. Aegir was (justifiably) annoyed by Thor's presumptuousness, so he told Thor that he would promise to brew them their beer only if they could fetch him a larger cauldron. Now Thor, not being a great strategist or problem solver, was at a loss for how to acquire a cauldron, but Tyr quietly went to Thor and suggested a secret plan. Tyr's father, a Jotun named Hymir, owned a cauldron that was a mile deep—the biggest cauldron ever known. Thor asked if they would be able to borrow this impressive beer cauldron, and Tyr replied that "borrow" might not be the right word, but they could obtain it nonetheless.

Together, Tyr and Thor journeyed for an entire day. They left Thor's goats with a farmer named Egil, and when they finally arrived at Hymir's house, they encountered two women. The first was Tyr's grandmother, an altogether unpleasant and ugly woman with nine hundred heads who showed no kindness to her grandson. But the second woman was Tyr's lovely mother, a concubine of Hymir's who warmly greeted them and brought beer. She offered to hide them from Hymir under one of the large cauldrons, knowing full well his reputation for being rude to unexpected guests, but when Hymir returned late from a fishing trip, she welcomed him home and announced Tyr and Thor's presence.

Hymir angrily busted through his own wall trying to find them, breaking eight of his own cauldrons in the process. Tyr and Thor emerged, and Hymir knew that according to customs of hospitality, he had no choice but to feed the guests under his roof, though he was far from happy about his son's choice in friends. He slaughtered three bulls and cooked them for dinner, but Thor (with his insatiable appetite) ate two whole bulls himself. Hymir realized that feeding Thor would be quite expensive, so he suggested they go fishing the next day.

You'll learn more about this intense fishing trip in the Midgard Serpent entry in Part 3, but for now, you just need to know that Hymir caught three tasty whales, and otherwise this fishing trip with Thor did *not* go as expected. Hymir lost more of his oxen, and in his anger, he insisted on testing Thor's strength. Back home, Hymir challenged Thor to break his glass cup. Thor threw the cup clear through the wall, but it was retrieved unbroken. Tyr's mother then whispered to Thor to smash the cup against Hymir's head, and sure enough, his hard head was unharmed but the cup shattered. Disappointed at the state of his broken glassware, Tyr's father told them that they could have the cauldron, and it seemed like clever Tyr's plan all along was to have the obnoxious Thor annoy the abrasive Hymir until he finally just relented and gave them what they wanted. Tyr tried twice to lift the cauldron but failed.

Luckily for Tyr, no one was stronger than Thor, and though his feet broke through the floorboards under the weight of the cauldron, Thor was able to lift it and carry it away. They retrieved Thor's goats, but one was limping, and Thor enslaved Egil's two children in retaliation for injuring the goat. As they walked home, they looked behind them and saw that Hymir was following them with an army of multiheaded Jotun bent on killing them (probably because Hymir now had a wrecked house and no beer). A battle ensued, the Jotun ended up dead, and Thor and Tyr returned to Asgard with the giant cauldron, where Aegir brewed them their beer as promised, which the gods drank and enjoyed.

MIMIR

ALSO KNOWN AS: MÍMIR, MÍMR, MIM
OLD NORSE TRANSLATION: "THE REMEMBERER"
KEY FAMILY MEMBERS: PERHAPS A RELATIVE OF ODIN

Mimir is best known for being the namesake, keeper, and guardian of the Well of Mimir, or the Spring of Wisdom, described in the *Gylfaginning* section of the Prose Edda as a well located beneath the roots of Yggdrasil. Mimir accumulated and sustained his immense wisdom and knowledge by drinking the water from this well daily, using his special drinking horn, called Gjallarhorn. Mimir enters the mythology as a character present during the Aesir-Vanir War and exists in a rather unique state: as a disembodied head that gives advice.

Not much has been detailed about Mimir's origin or family history, but through studying the use of poetic devices called "kennings" (references that are substituted for other words throughout the poems in the Poetic Edda), some Old Norse scholars believe that Mimir was the brother of Bestla, the Jotun from the creation myth who was Odin's mother, which would make him Odin's uncle. Whether he was Odin's uncle or simply his friend, the intelligent Mimir is described and referenced primarily through his connection to Odin, who simply couldn't get enough of his wisdom, advice, and trivia.

THE STORY YOU NEED TO KNOW:

After the fallout of the Aesir-Vanir War, peace was accomplished through the exchange of hostages. The Vanir father-son duo Njord and Frey were sent to the Aesir, and with them went Freyja—hence their presence in Asgard rather than Vanaheim throughout the stories in the mythology. As we see with this Vanir family, and with the emphasis on wisdom in the other hostages, the goal seems to have been that these hostages would integrate into the opposite society as active participants and both sides would have the opportunity to learn from each other.

Slightly less is known of Hoenir and Mimir, the Aesir who were sent as hostages to the Vanir. According to Snorri in *Ynglinga Saga* in *Heimskringla*, Njord and Frey were exchanged for Hoenir, who was so handsome and strong that the Vanir elected him to be their new leader. Mimir was exchanged for Kvasir, the wisest of all the Vanir. But eventually, the Vanir realized that it was in fact Mimir who was telling their new leader Hoenir everything he knew, and they deemed the whole exchange unfair. They had given up Kvasir the wise and the wealthy and attractive Njord and Frey (with a bonus sister thrown in!), and they had received only the handsome but otherwise useless Hoenir and his advisor Mimir in return. To express their discontent with the exchange in no uncertain terms, the Vanir decided they would behead Mimir and send his decapitated head back to Odin.

Snorri tells us in *Ynglinga Saga* in *Heimskringla* that Odin went so far as to preserve Mimir's head with herbs and enchant

it with spells so that Mimir could continue to speak and reveal advice and secrets to him upon request. Based on various references throughout the text, coded in kennings—especially in the stories that describe Ragnarok—it seems that Odin frequently carried Mimir's preserved head around with him, or else kept it somewhere where it was easily accessible, so that he could consult with Mimir when he needed advice, wisdom, or knowledge.

In *Voluspa* in the Poetic Edda, as well as in the *Gylfaginning* section of the Prose Edda, we also learn that Odin deposited his eye in Mimir's well in exchange for a drink of the water.

Now You Know

Animal horns have been used as tools by humans for many purposes. In the Viking era and Middle Ages of Scandinavia, and often reflected in the Eddas and sagas, common uses included both drinking horns and musical instrument horns—and some horns could be used for both. At some point, Mimir's drinking horn Gjallarhorn ("loud horn") ended up in the hands of Heimdall, whose beverage of choice was mead rather than wisdom-water. The horn served a double function as both a vessel for mead and a noisemaker, as Heimdall would eventually blow upon Gjallarhorn as a warning call to the other gods, letting them know that Ragnarok had begun to unfold.

ITHUNN AND BRAGI

ALSO KNOWN AS: IÐUNN, IDUNN
OLD NORSE TRANSLATION: "EVER-YOUNG"; "THE POET"
KEY FAMILY MEMBERS: EACH OTHER!

Ithunn and Bragi were a married couple who frequently conversed with the other Aesir, but they do not often appear as active characters in the stories. However, they had very important jobs. If not for Ithunn, the gods would've quickly wearied of their wars and adventures; and if not for Bragi, the gods may not have maintained a record of their glorious feats and victories. Ithunn was the goddess who grew and tended the magic apples that the gods ate to maintain their eternal youth. Her husband, Bragi, was the foremost skald, or poet, renowned for his skill with words and wisdom.

THE STORY YOU NEED TO KNOW:

While Bragi himself was a storyteller, he doesn't have a story about himself. There is a story about Ithunn in *Skaldskaparmal* of the Prose Edda: It begins, as most problems do, with Loki. One day while they were out adventuring in the wilderness, Odin, Loki, and Hoenir became hungry and found an ox to slaughter for a snack. They made a fire pit and tried to cook the ox, but it would not cook. Up in the oak tree, they heard a voice, which turned out to be an eagle, who informed them that their meat would not cook without his help. In exchange for his rendering aid, though, they'd need to share their meal with him.

They accepted the eagle's help, and when the ox was done cooking, the eagle swooped down and gobbled up more than what Loki deemed was his fair share. So he grabbed a stick and threw it at the eagle, but it got stuck: They were now in a predicament because one end of the stick was stuck to the eagle, and the other to Loki's hands. The eagle flew up in the air, dragging Loki with him until he felt like his arms would be ripped off, all the while smashing his feet repeatedly into rocks and trees. Loki begged for a truce, and the eagle said that he would release Loki only if he promised to bring Ithunn and her magic apples out of the protected region of Asgard. Always the first to look out for himself, Loki agreed to the conditions and rejoined his companions as they returned to Asgard.

Loki found Ithunn and told her that he had found the most incredible apples in his ventures outside of the protected fortress of Asgard, and he told her she should follow him into the forest to find them and bring some of her own apples to compare. While she was searching for these apples, unsuspecting of any mischief, the eagle—who turned out to be the Jotun named Thiassi (the father of Skadi in our story about Njord) in disguise—swooped down and carried her off, along with her basket of apples, to his home in Thrymheim.

Meanwhile, the gods missed Ithunn and started to grow old without her apples, so they gathered to discuss what could have possibly caused her mysterious disappearance and where she

might be. Last anyone knew, she had gone out into the forest with Loki. So the gods brought Loki before them and threatened him with torture and death unless he could undo this damage and rescue Ithunn.

He borrowed Freyja's feather suit that turned him into a falcon, flew to Jotunheim, and found Ithunn had been left home alone in Thiassi's house while he was out at sea. Loki turned Ithunn into a nut, held her tightly in his falcon claws, and flew her home to Asgard as quickly as he could. But when Thiassi got home and realized his kidnapped goddess was missing, he turned back into an eagle and followed in hot pursuit. But the Aesir were ready for him: They saw the falcon flying fast and carrying a nut and recognized this as Loki and allowed him to drop down behind the protection of Asgard's fortified walls. As the Jotun-eagle sped toward the wall, they ignited a huge fire of wood shavings, but the eagle was going too fast to stop. He collided with the flames and scorched his wings, causing him to fall and lose his eagle shape and turn back into a Jotun. When he hit the ground, the Aesir quickly closed in and killed him as punishment for stealing Ithunn and their magic apples of eternal youth.

Now You Know

We encounter stories of women like Ithunn and troublesome apples in several mythologies and religions: Eris and the Apple of Discord that starts the Trojan War in Greek mythology, Eve and the Apple of Knowledge that gets her and Adam banished from the Garden of Eden in the Old Testament, even Snow White and the poisoned apple in much later European fairy tales. In these stories, apples are a source of conflict, either intentionally or accidentally, for the women who possess them. Considering fruits are common symbols of fertility, these tragic apples could be interpreted as allusions to the woman's own fertility: either her inherent value to her husband and society via her youthfulness and ability to bear children (like Ithunn and Snow White) or her femininity and sexuality as a dangerous temptation (Eve's tempting of Adam to eat the apple, or Aphrodite's promise to give the already-married Helen of Sparta as a wife to Paris of Troy in exchange for the Apple of Discord). Likewise, these apple-inspired conflicts could resonate with deeply rooted and widespread societal fears surrounding women's sexuality.

PART 3

THE JOTUN AND OTHER VILLAINS

There are many troublemakers in the Norse mythology that keep the Aesir and Vanir on their toes. However, like the moral code of the gods, the concept of villainy is also a bit complicated. For example, some villains, like Loki, have both positive and negative interactions with the Aesir, and while the Jotun are considered the primary villains of the mythology, several of them intermarry and have children with the Aesir and Vanir, living among them in apparent harmony. By contrast, there are stories where gods like Thor demonstrate absolutely no qualms about killing Jotun for inconveniencing him, even in just the slightest way, because their assumed "enemy" status justifies their deaths.

Perhaps you've heard the word "giant" associated with the primary villains in Old Norse myths, like the Frost Giants of Jotunheim in the Marvel universe of Thor? "Giant" is often how we translate "Jotun" from Old Norse into English, but it's more accurate to call them Jotun (the "j" is pronounced like a "y") because the Jotun/giants aren't actually bigger than the Aesir or Vanir, just a different society or faction (modern-day Old Norse scholar Jackson Crawford refers to them as "anti-gods").

But the Jotun aren't the only villains the Aesir have to worry about—we'll meet some other remarkable creatures too! There are a few shady human characters in this part, as well as an assortment of supernatural monsters, a dwarf, and a big, bad wolf. Additionally, we'll explore just how morally ambiguous the Aesir and Vanir can be sometimes. While Loki fits squarely in the category of "antagonist," other characters who you *thought* were "good guys" might in fact get a kick out of being irritating to their friends and family, just for the fun of it.

LOKI

ALSO KNOWN AS: **LOKE, LOPT**
OLD NORSE TRANSLATION: **POSSIBLY "KNOT-TANGLER"**
KEY FAMILY MEMBERS: **WIFE SIGYN; CHILDREN FENRIR,
JORMUNGAND, AND HEL**

Loki is arguably the most enigmatic character in Norse mythology. Sometimes, he coexists among the Aesir and Vanir as a hot-headed friend whose cunning is helpful in resolving conflicts (like in *Thrymskvitha*, our story about Freyja), while other times, he is a villain leaving behind a trail of destruction and lamentation (such as killing Balder and fighting against the Aesir and Vanir during Ragnarok). And yet other stories present Loki's personality as somewhere in-between: a nuisance who is nonetheless allowed to remain among the gods in Asgard. Like many devilish figures in mythologies around the world, this trickster has a handsome face that almost hides his mean streak.

Loki also boasts one of the more...unorthodox family trees in the mythology. Unlike in the Marvel universe, he was not a relative (adopted or otherwise) of Odin and Thor. According to *Gylfaginning* in the Prose Edda, his parents were Jotun: His father was Farbauti, and his mother was named either Laufey or Nal. His wife was Sigyn, and they had a son together named

Narfi. But Loki also procreated with a Jotun named Angrboda, and those children were a bit more unusual: a wolf named Fenrir, a serpent named Jormungand (the Midgard Serpent), and a goddess named Hel. Loki tried to hide these three children in Jotunheim, but the Aesir found them, and fearing the prophecies of Ragnarok, they attempted to restrain Fenrir and the serpent and sent Hel to administer to the underworld, also called Hel.

But Loki's list of offspring doesn't end there. In the poem *Voluspa en skamma* from the Poetic Edda, we learn that he bore a couple more children himself. While disguised as a mare (he was a frequent shape-shifter), Loki was impregnated by the stallion Svathilfari, and in this form he gave birth to Odin's eight-legged horse Sleipnir. Loki also found and ate a dead woman's heart, which again made him pregnant, and he birthed another child from whom all troll women were later descended.

THE STORY YOU NEED TO KNOW:

Loki appears in many stories, but the poem that is named for him in the Poetic Edda is *Lokasenna.* It explains how conflicted his relationships with the Aesir and Vanir really were, and how much he relished being a source of irritation and genuine grief. In this story, Aegir hosted a feast for the gods after preparing an ale in a great cauldron stolen from Hymir (see more about this story in the Tyr entry in Part 2). All was peaceful and bright while beer was served. However, Loki was jealous to hear the gods compliment Aegir's servants, and so he killed the servant Fimafeng. The other gods kicked him out, but he talked his way back in.

The first person he met at the door was a servant named Eldir, who told Loki that no one was feeling particularly friendly toward him and he'd better go away. But Loki insisted on returning, and everyone fell silent as he reentered and requested a drink. Bragi told him to leave, but Loki then reminded Odin of an oath he had made to not drink if Loki was not also served. Either because he wanted to finish his beer or wanted to honor his oaths (or both), Odin told his son Vidar to yield his seat to Loki and get him a drink. Loki then made a toast to the assembly of gods—all except Bragi, who he called out for making him unwelcome.

Bragi warned Loki against slander, which is of course exactly what Loki did next. Some of his insults were subjective and predictable, but others referencing specific events were not mentioned elsewhere and could simply have been lies to incite scandal. One by one he insulted them, first calling Bragi a coward. When Ithunn tried to break the two up, Loki accused her of being lustful and sleeping with her brother's murderer (but did Ithunn even have a brother?). Loki then accused Odin of having poor judgment when granting victories in battle, and Odin called out Loki's gender-bending tendencies to try to shame him in return. When Frigg tried to calm Odin, Loki turned on her next, accusing her of sleeping with her brothers-in-law, Vili and Ve (according to Snorri's *Ynglinga Saga* in *Heimskringla*, Vili and Ve might have claimed her, along with all of Odin's other "possessions," when Odin once ventured so far they thought he'd never return), which sounds like victim-blaming to me. In response to Loki, Frigg stated:

"You know, if I had a son
Like Balder, sitting here
With me in Aegir's hall,
In the presence of these gods,
I declare you would never come out
Alive, you'd be killed shortly."

(Jackson Crawford's translation, *The Poetic Edda:
Stories of the Norse Gods and Heroes*, copyright © 2015)

Loki then had the audacity to remind her of the role he played in Balder's death, at which point Freyja interjected that he must be crazy to insult Frigg in this way. As with the other goddesses, Loki responded by slut-shaming Freyja, accusing her of having slept with every guest present, including her own brother (the Vanir do have a reputation for incest). Her father, Njord, then tried to defend her. (Though it was not a great defense—the best he could come up with was, "It's none of Loki's business if women decide to commit incest.") Loki responded by reminding Njord of the time he let some Jotun women urinate in his mouth (eww) and when he fathered Frey with his own sister (also eww, but quite possibly true).

Tyr defended Frey as being an upstanding guy despite his parentage, but Loki taunted Tyr, claiming that he had slept with Tyr's wife (did Tyr have a wife?). This heated banter continued until Sif offered Loki a drink, begging him not to insult her as he had the others. Nonetheless, he accused her of being unfaithful to her husband, Thor, and Loki should know—it might have been Loki himself that she cheated with.

Suddenly, the earth trembled, and Thor returned from his adventures. He told Loki to shut up or else he'd let Mjolnir shut him up by way of knocking his head off his shoulders. Thor and Loki exchanged a few more insults, and finally, Loki left, shape-shifting into a salmon to escape. But the gods caught him and tied him to the rock under the venom-dripping serpent as punishment for both his confessed role in Balder's murder and his defamation of the gods and goddesses. Eventually, though, we know he would escape this torture and fulfill his destiny as the primary instigator and antagonist at the coming of Ragnarok.

HEL

OLD NORSE TRANSLATION: **"CONCEALED PLACE"**
KEY FAMILY MEMBERS: **FATHER LOKI**

Hel was the daughter of Loki and a personification of death, a goddess who got her name from the underworld she administered. She was banished by Odin to be the guardian of the underworld, also called Hel, when it was discovered that Loki had sired the children that were prophesized to destroy the gods at Ragnarok. Both fierce and morose, she was described as being half-flesh-colored and half-black—not due to melanin or natural pigmentation of her skin, but rather that she was half-alive and half-corpse. She had a dog named Garm who guarded the gates of the underworld, which was either presented as a separate realm (as in the Poetic Edda's *Grimnismal*) or on the ice world of Niflheim (as Snorri reports in *Gylfaginning* in the Prose Edda). Wherever Hel may have been in relation to the other worlds, Hel the goddess was tasked with providing lodging and care for all the people who were sent to her realm, which means she was probably quite busy. Snorri tells us the walls were high around her hall (called "Eliudnir"), where the entryway threshold was called "Stumbling Block," her bed was called "Sick Bed," her dish was called "Hunger," and her knife was called "Famine."

As unpleasant as hunger and famine may sound, Hel was not thought of as being a place of pain and punishment, which would be easy to assume given the similarity of its name to the Christian hell. Afterlife with Hel in Hel instead seems to have been relatively peaceful and restful (unless you were a Volva and people kept waking you up to chat!). This was the afterlife waiting for everyone who did not die in combat only to be escorted to Valhalla by the Valkyries. Broadly speaking, those whose souls went to Hel after death included women, children, elderly people, and anyone who died of illness, accident, or natural causes.

THE STORY YOU NEED TO KNOW:

Hel is an often-referenced character, but she is elusive. People talk about her in the context of death (for example, they would say that Hel would take their fallen enemy, or they would mention riding to Hel with no distinction between the place or goddess who lived there), but we rarely see or hear from her directly—in fact, not at all in the Poetic Edda. This leads some Old Norse scholars to wonder, was she actually a character in the pre-Christian beliefs—or was she a personification of the place that emerged only in the later thirteenth-century versions of the stories recorded by Christians, like Snorri, who might have mistaken some of the place references for a goddess?

One way or another, by the time of Snorri's writing, she was a goddess, and she does have a role in the Prose Edda's story surrounding Balder. Following his death and elaborate funeral in *Gylfaginning*, yet another son of Odin and half-brother of Balder named Hermod rode for nine days and nights through the darkest valleys until he came to a river named Gioll with a bridge guarded by a woman named Modgud. She asked him who he was and how he could thunder across the bridge so loudly, making more noise than the five battalions of dead soldiers that had crossed just the other day—surely, he didn't look like a dead man! Hermod told her that he was alive and searching for Balder on the road to Hel. Modgud informed him that Balder had indeed passed this way and gave him directions to go to Hel.

Hermod finally arrived and found Balder sitting on a throne in high honor. He spent the night there, and in the morning, he begged Hel to release Balder, telling her of the ceaseless mourning in Asgard. She decided that this must be tested: If Balder really was so beloved, surely Hermod could convince all living things—and all dead things too—to weep for Balder. Balder gave Hermod Odin's ring Draupnir, which had been set on his funeral pyre with him, as a gift to return to Odin, and Nanna, Balder's wife, sent Hermod with gifts of linen and jewelry for Frigg and her handmaiden Fulla. Then Hermod returned to Asgard and reported what had been done, and the gods set out to make everything weep for Balder. And all things wept—all the people, animals, rocks, and trees—until they came to a cave and found, sitting alone, a Jotun woman named Thanks (who is suspected to be Loki in disguise). They asked her to weep for Balder, but she could not, saying, "No good got I from the old one's son either dead or alive. Let Hel hold what she has." (Anthony Faulkes's translation, *Edda*, copyright © 1987.) Thus, Balder had to remain with Hel, and in the *Skaldskaparmal* section of the Prose Edda, he is referred to in kennings as "Hel's companion."

Now You Know

In Saxo Grammaticus's text recounting the history of the kings of Denmark, *The History of the Danes*, he tries to connect historical kings with mythical gods in more tangible ways, requiring significant changes to some of the stories. In his version, the goddess of death is involved in Balder's story even earlier, visiting Balder in his dreams to give him forewarning that he will be sent to her embrace. But that's not the only difference between Saxo and the other accounts of Balder's death—Saxo's very unusual account recasts Balder and Hod as mortal brothers fighting for the love of Nanna, and this jealousy causes Hod to stab Balder to death.

THE MIDGARD SERPENT

ALSO KNOWN AS: **THE WORLD SERPENT, JORMUNGAND, JÖRMUNGAND**

OLD NORSE TRANSLATION: **"HUGE MONSTER"**

KEY FAMILY MEMBERS: **FATHER LOKI**

The Midgard Serpent was a giant dragon or snake-like monster that lived in the deepest depths of the ocean and encircled the world of humans. Fathered by Loki with a Jotun woman named Angrboda, the serpent was thrown into the sea by Odin after he discovered Loki's unusual children. Odin hoped to keep the serpent out of trouble by banishing it to the ocean floor. As the defender of and frequent adventurer in Midgard, Thor was the god who tangled most with the Midgard Serpent, and they would be the doom of each other at Ragnarok. Unlike other animals in the mythology, the Midgard Serpent is never described anthropomorphically: It doesn't have a reputation for speaking or listening to human language like Fenrir or the many bird messengers throughout the stories—so at the very least, it seems that if the serpent could speak, it chose not to. Rather, the Midgard

Serpent was a carnal beast, preferring to use its mouth for constant devouring instead of talking.

THE STORY YOU NEED TO KNOW:

In Part 2, Tyr's story explained how he and Thor ventured off together to find a Jotun named Hymir and acquire a pot large enough to brew beer in for all the gods. While Thor and Tyr were staying with Hymir long enough to win his cauldron, Hymir asked Thor to accompany him on a fishing trip so that they would have more food and Thor wouldn't eat through his entire herd of oxen. Thor agreed, offered to row the boat himself, and asked for some bait, but Hymir didn't feel like sharing. Thor then improvised and ripped the head off yet another of Hymir's oxen, then used the entire ox head as bait, earning Hymir's emphatic disapproval (but the scene is so iconic that images of Thor fishing with an ox head appear frequently in Viking-era artwork). Hymir caught three whales, but Thor, with his massive bait, caught the Midgard Serpent instead! He kept pulling on the line, trying to get the serpent in the boat so that he could kill it, but it was huge and had poisonous breath.

According to *Hymiskvitha*, Thor smashed the serpent in the head with his hammer and the monster erupted in anger and agony, causing the ocean and earth to shake, before sinking back down to the bottom of the sea. They then paddled home, Thor upset about losing his shot at the serpent and Hymir probably jealous that Thor's catch was far more impressive than his own. At Hymir's request for one more favor, Thor helped him tie up the boat by lifting it up, full of water and all, and carrying it through the forest back to Hymir's house.

Snorri tells the second half of the fishing story a bit differently in *Gylfaginning* in the Prose Edda: When the Midgard Serpent started to pull on Thor's fishing line, Thor braced himself with such strength that his feet went crashing through the boat and hit the sea floor. When Thor succeeded in reeling in and pulling up the monster and Hymir looked into the gaping mouth of the serpent as it wrestled with Thor, the Jotun went into a complete and total panic. Instead of waiting, staying out of the way, and letting Thor fight his arch nemesis, Hymir, in his cowardice, took a knife and cut Thor's fishing line right before he could strike the serpent. Thus, he let it slip free and return to the depths of the sea, robbing Thor of his potential victory over his fated doom. Thor threw Mjolnir into the water after it, and it's said that he struck it in the head, but he did not kill the serpent. Angry at Hymir for depriving him of his catch, Thor then boxed Hymir across the ears so hard that he went flying into the water headfirst. Thor waded ashore, leaving Hymir to find his own way home with his now broken and water-logged boat.

Now You Know

The Midgard Serpent is an example of an ouroboros, a serpent
or similar creature that eats its own tail and essentially comes
full circle, thereby embodying the complete circle of life
(so it's fitting that the word has so many *o*'s in it). The word
"ouroboros" originates from Greek, and this creature appears
in many mythologies around the world. It's often interpreted
cross-culturally as a symbol of death and rebirth, not unlike
the descriptions of the destruction and re-creation of the
universe that will follow Ragnarok. So, while all the Norse talk
about the death of the gods may seem gloomy, built into the
mythological world and its structure are hints that at some
point after the end, a rebirth is imminent.

FENRIR

ALSO KNOWN AS: **FENRISÚLFR**

OLD NORSE TRANSLATION: **"THE FENRIS WOLF"**

KEY FAMILY MEMBERS: **FATHER LOKI**

Fenrir the wolf was the final child of Loki and Angrboda, brother to the goddess Hel and the Midgard Serpent. Some scholars think that Fenrir and Hel's guard dog Garm were at one point the same creature, but eventually these names were split into separate canine characters. Fated to be the death of Odin, Fenrir would eventually break free of all bondage and devour Odin during the battle of Ragnarok, but Odin's son Vidar would avenge his father by killing the wolf.

THE STORY YOU NEED TO KNOW:

Snorri tells the story of the fettering of Fenrir in the *Gylfaginning* section of the Prose Edda. Fearing the prophecies of Ragnarok and the fact that Loki's children might turn out to be just as much trouble as their father, the gods went to Jotunheim in search of Fenrir and his siblings. But while Hel was banished to care for the dead and the Midgard Serpent was sent to the bottom of the sea, there was no convenient place for the Aesir to imprison Fenrir, and so they did perhaps the least wise thing they could possibly

have done with him: They took him home to Asgard and tried to raise him there. Snorri doesn't tell us why the Aesir decided this, but it could be because they were out of ideas or because Odin was quite partial to wolves due to their association with war and carrion—though it would be a bit out of character for him to take this chance since he was otherwise desperately trying to prevent Ragnarok and save himself. Snorri does tell us that they could not kill Fenrir because they didn't want to defile their sanctuary in Asgard with Fenrir's blood.

Regardless of their rationale, the Aesir now had a hungry baby wolf to raise. Only the god Tyr was brave enough to approach and feed Fenrir, and much to their dismay, this baby wolf quickly grew up to be a big, strong, angry adult wolf. So, the Aesir devised a clever plan to try and restrain Fenrir, and perhaps minimize the damage he was destined to cause. The gods forged a strong fetter (a chain or shackle) called "Leyding." They brought this fetter to Fenrir and asked if he would like to test his growing strength. Fenrir took one look at the fetter and determined it was no match for him. He allowed himself to be shackled, and with one kick he managed to break loose. The gods built another fetter twice as strong called "Dromi," and promised him he would earn a great reputation of strength if he could manage to bust out of this one. Fenrir decided that such fame would be worth the risk, and so he allowed the gods to restrain him again. With a few kicks and shakes, he strained against Dromi until it shattered and sent iron shrapnel flying in all directions.

At this point, the Aesir were getting nervous. What if they could no longer restrain this fearsome wolf-child of Loki's? Frey sent his messenger Skirnir to the realm of the dwarves (or dark elves), known to be great builders and smiths, and Skirnir asked them to construct the strongest fetter possible for Fenrir. The dwarves constructed this fetter using some unusual ingredients: the sound of a cat's paws as it runs, the beard of a woman, the roots of a mountain, a bear's sinew, a fish's breath, and a bird's spittle. These six ingredients produced a fetter that was silky smooth and soft, and yet hard and strong. Skirnir brought this new fetter, called "Gleipnir," to the Aesir, and they decided they would go to an island called "Lyngvi," in the middle of a lake called "Amsvartnir," and challenge Fenrir again.

The gods showed Fenrir the fetter, taking turns trying to break it themselves, each of them failing. Fenrir took one look at Gleipnir, no wider or stronger-looking than a ribbon, and said that there was no fame or glory to be had in tearing a ribbon, but he was suspicious that some magic or trickery had been involved in its creation. The gods told him that if he refused to break the ribbon, they would free him for being so weak and cowardly, and they would never fear him again. Fenrir absolutely did not want to lose his reputation as a terrifying big, bad wolf, so he negotiated a compromise: To prove that the gods issued this challenge in good faith, one of them was to put their hand in his mouth as he allowed himself to be tied with Gleipnir.

Who would be brave enough to accept such a compromise? The one-handed god Tyr, of course—who, up until this point, had two hands. The ribbon was tied around Fenrir's legs, and as he kicked and struggled against it, the fetter only grew stronger. When he realized he had been tricked, the angry wolf ripped off Tyr's right hand. He continued to struggle while the Aesir laughed at the wolf's confinement (except Tyr, who was definitely *not* laughing) and anchored Gleipnir to the ground with giant rocks so that Fenrir was firmly stuck. As he tried to bite them, they thrust a giant sword in his mouth, the hilt braced against his lower fangs and the point digging into his upper gums, and in this state of imprisonment he would howl while a river of saliva ran from his mouth (the river they named "Hope") until the coming of Ragnarok, when Fenrir would finally break free of Gleipnir and join his father, Loki, in bringing about chaos, death, and destruction.

KING GEIRROTH

ALSO KNOWN AS: GEIRROD, GEIRROÐ
OLD NORSE TRANSLATION: POSSIBLY "PEACE BY SPEAR"
KEY FAMILY MEMBERS: BROTHER AGNAR; SON AGNAR

King Geirroth was not a Jotun or supernatural villain, but rather a mortal man who found himself up against Odin in a test—not of strength or wit, but of hospitality—and ended up wronging him. Being a good host was of paramount importance in Viking society, and people of all socioeconomic classes were expected to be courteous and welcoming to travelers in need. This story, from *Grimnismal* in the Poetic Edda, illustrates why: You never know when the ragged-looking guest at your door might in fact be Odin in disguise, and your fate may hinge on how well you treat him. We also learn in this story that Odin was not the only Aesir who played games with the lives and deaths of mortals.

THE STORY YOU NEED TO KNOW:

There once was a king named Hrauthung who had two sons named Agnar (age ten) and Geirroth (age eight). These two boys set out on a fishing trip, but the wind blew their boat far away, and in the dark they wrecked on a strange land where they were taken in and fostered by a poor farmer and his wife. The wife took special care of Agnar, and the farmer took it upon himself to educate Geirroth. The following spring, the couple gave the boys a new boat and sent them back home. As they approached their father's kingdom, Geirroth quickly jumped ashore and shoved the boat back out to sea with Agnar still in it, cursing him to go wherever the trolls might take him. Upon returning home, Geirroth learned that their father was dead, and in the absence of his older brother he was made king.

Time passed and both boys grew to be men. But they didn't know that the farmer and his wife were Odin and Frigg in disguise or that they would be caught in a competition between the god and goddess—which Odin thought he had won since Geirroth (whom he tutored) was now a great king, while Agnar (whom Frigg looked after) was now living in a cave having children with a troll woman. But Frigg told Odin that Geirroth was not so great a king, since rumors said he starved his guests and was stingy in matters of hospitality. Odin did not believe the rumor and made a bet with his wife that he could prove these accusations against his foster son were a lie.

Unbeknownst to Odin, Frigg sent her handmaiden Fulla to Geirroth to deliver a warning that a great sorcerer was afoot and could be recognized by the fact that no dogs would attack him. In so doing, Frigg outsmarted her husband and turned the rumor into a self-fulfilling prophecy. While Geirroth was not, in fact, in the habit of starving his guests before, he was now extremely leery of this sorcerer and ordered any man who wasn't attacked by dogs to be apprehended and brought before him. A man appeared in the kingdom, wearing a long cloak and traveling under the name Shadow-Face, and the dogs didn't go near him.

And so, Odin—going by the name Shadow-Face—was captured and brought to Geirroth's hall. Suspecting this Shadow-Face to be the sorcerer who Fulla had warned him about, Geirroth interrogated and tortured Odin, trying to extract information from him; but Odin told him nothing except this false name. Geirroth then tied his visitor up between two fires and left him there with no food or drink for eight nights. The king's son, named Agnar after his uncle, knew this was obviously no way to treat a guest. The young boy went behind his father's back to Shadow-Face and offered him a drinking horn, just as the fires were growing so large that they started to burn Odin's cloak.

Odin cursed the fire and told Agnar that he would be well repaid for a single drink. He promised to make Agnar the sole ruler of all his father's lands and gave him a fair amount of education as an additional reward. Odin told Agnar of the names and halls of all the gods, as well as the rivers and realms of Yggdrasil, and described the making of the universe. He named his Valkyries, horses, wolves, and ravens, and gave Agnar a partial but still extensive list of the disguises and names he had gone by in his many travels among the humans. He finally identified himself to be Odin and declared that Geirroth had made himself drunk and unwise and had lost the god's favor.

As Geirroth heard this, he immediately regretted hanging this guest up between the two fire pits and drew his sword to release Odin's bondage. But he suddenly dropped his sword and it fell, the hilt hitting the ground and the blade pointing up, just as the king himself tripped and accidentally impaled himself through the chest. Under these strangely coincidental circumstances Geirroth died, and his son Agnar was made king as Odin promised.

Odin then went on his merry way, feeling that justice had been served to Geirroth and not giving a second thought to Agnar (the uncle), who was still living in a cave with trolls while his ten-year-old nephew ruled the kingdom.

SUTTUNG, BAUGI, AND GUNNLOD

OLD NORSE TRANSLATION: "HEAVY WITH DRINK";
"RING-SHAPED"; "INVITATION TO BATTLE"
KEY FAMILY MEMBERS: EACH OTHER

Suttung, Baugi, and Gunnlod were the Jotun family from whom Odin stole the Mead of Poetry, a magical beverage that brought wisdom and eloquence to the drinker in addition to being delicious. Suttung and Baugi were brothers, and Gunnlod was Suttung's daughter. Their story paints a clear picture of the natural animosity and social hierarchies between the Jotun and the Aesir. While these characters never really did anything to offend Odin personally, he still felt like he deserved what they had and was justified to acquire it by any means necessary—because he was the boss.

THE STORY YOU NEED TO KNOW:

In *Skaldskaparmal* in the Prose Edda, Snorri writes this story as told by Bragi, the poet of the Aesir, to a man named Aegir, a practiced magician who traveled to Asgard to feast with the gods.

Bragi tells him that the gods all spit in a vat to seal their truce and mark the resolution of the Aesir-Vanir War. From their saliva was born a god named Kvasir, but he was later killed by two dwarves named Fialar and Galar. They poured out his blood and mixed it with honey, and when it fermented into mead, whoever drank the mead became a great poet and scholar, and this became known as the Mead of Poetry.

Fialar and Galar traveled about and lodged one night with a Jotun named Gilling and his wife. When Gilling invited the dwarves out on a boat with him—in another Norse mythology fishing trip that doesn't go according to plan—the dwarves capsized the boat, and Gilling drowned. His wife was so upset that she didn't stop wailing, and when Fialar offered to take her to the place where her husband drowned so that she might console herself and find peace, Galar hid above her door and dropped a millstone on her head, killing her. Unbeknownst to Fialar and Galar, Gilling had a son named Suttung, who was now quite angry with the dwarves. To atone for killing his parents, they offered him the Mead of Poetry, which Suttung accepted as repayment. He hid the Mead of Poetry in a secret place called "Hnitbiorg," where his daughter Gunnlod was charged with guarding it.

Odin of course knew about such things from his high seat in Asgard, and he decided that in addition to hanging himself from Yggdrasil and giving his eye to the Well of Mimir, he also needed a sip of this Mead of Poetry. Odin came across nine enslaved people mowing hay and offered to sharpen their scythes. He threw his whetstone in the air, and they all tried to catch it; but in the process, all nine of them accidentally cut each other's throats, and they died in a heap.

Odin went to Baugi, the farmer who owned these enslaved people, and under the false name Bolverk ("Evil-Doer") offered to make up the workload of his nine missing workers in exchange for a drink of his brother Suttung's special mead. Baugi said that he had no influence over Suttung and no control over who tasted the mead, but he offered to try. Baugi inquired after a drink for his new friend Bolverk, but Suttung refused. This of course angered Odin, so he told Baugi to bore a hole through Suttung's mountain. The first time, Baugi tried to cheat Bolverk; but Odin realized that the tunnel didn't go all the way through the mountain and made him drill again. The second time, Baugi did as he was told, and Odin transformed himself into a snake and slithered his way through the mountain, narrowly avoiding Baugi's attempts to stab him with his auger.

Once he arrived on the other side and landed in Suttung's dwelling, he saw Suttung's daughter Gunnlod guarding the Mead of Poetry. He seduced her for three nights, and each night, she let him drink a cupful of mead, until he drank it all. And then, without further ado, Odin left Gunnlod in the lurch and transformed himself into an eagle, flying away back to Asgard as quickly as he could. When he realized what had transpired, Suttung also transformed into an eagle and followed. The hot pursuit continued until Odin reached Asgard, where the gods held out containers so Odin could spit out the mead when he flew past. The chase between Odin and Suttung was so close that in his distress, Odin "sent some of the mead out backwards," as Anthony Faulkes describes in his 1987 translation, *Edda*. This mead was not included in the containers being saved by the other Aesir because it wasn't regurgitated mead—it actually sounds more like urinated mead—and the gods had standards, after all. Odin narrowly escaped, and he shared the regurgitated Mead of Poetry with any of the Aesir who wished to try some, and those who drank it became great poets. This is how Odin became the god of poetry.

Now You Know

In some kennings, Bragi is called "son of Odin." Now, many gods are referred to in kennings as sons of Odin, and that could be because he was their leader or because he was their actual father. Since he impregnated so many women, it's very difficult to keep track of all his sons. We don't know for sure who Bragi's mother was or if Odin really was his father. But some scholars think perhaps he was the son of Odin and Gunnlod, conceived during their three nights of seduction and mead-drinking. And it would make sense: The Aesir's chief poet could be the product of a union between these two characters who are both heavily associated with poetry.

HRUNGNIR

Hrungnir was a legendary adversary of the Aesir, appearing in references throughout the Poetic and Prose Eddas. He embodies many of the qualities of a typical Jotun character who angers and offends the gods: He was arrogant, boastful, and entitled; not a well-behaved guest; and derived great joy from antagonizing Odin and Thor especially.

THE STORY YOU NEED TO KNOW:

Snorri combines several episodes into one story in *Skaldskaparmal* in the Prose Edda, which encapsulates Hrungnir's role in the myths. It begins with Odin riding his eight-legged horse Sleipnir through Jotunheim, while Thor was occupied elsewhere killing trolls. Wearing his golden helmet and galloping across the sea and sky on his magnificent horse, Odin captured Hrungnir's attention, and Hrungnir asked who this man was on such an impressive steed. Odin affirmed that his horse was the best, and wagered his head on a bet that no horse of Jotunheim could possibly win a race against Sleipnir. Hrungnir accepted the challenge, believing his horse Gullfaxi could outrun Sleipnir. And so

the race began, with Odin and Sleipnir taking the lead, and they raced hard and fast until Hrungnir in his blind fury raced Odin all the way to Asgard and right through the front gates. Odin won the race, but being a good sport about it, he invited Hrungnir to join the gods for a drink.

Hrungnir accepted the invitation, entering the hall and demanding his promised drink. He drank and drank until he became intoxicated and foolish. In his overconfident drunkenness, he started to brag and threaten the Aesir. He vowed to take the whole hall back to Jotunheim, destroy all of Asgard, and kill all gods except for Freyja and Sif, whom he would carry off with him and presumably rape. Freyja was the only cupbearer brave enough to continue bringing him the drinks he demanded, and he continued boasting that he would not stop until he drank all of the Aesir's ale. At this point, the gods had had just about enough of Hrungnir's threats and rudeness, and they summoned Thor, who always showed up just in the nick of time when there was mischief in Asgard.

Thor burst through the door with Mjolnir at the ready and demanded to know why Freyja was bringing this Jotun drinks in Thor's cup, in the Aesir's hall, and why such a horrible guest was allowed in Asgard (some sources infer that Thor was especially angry because Hrungnir had at one point kidnapped Thor's daughter). Hrungnir responded that it was Odin who had invited him, and as Odin's guest, he was under his protection. And besides, Hrungnir came unarmed—it wouldn't be honorable for Thor to kill an unarmed man who was drinking and feasting at Odin's invitation.

Thor vowed to make Hrungnir regret ever accepting the invitation and challenged him to combat. Hrungnir returned to Jotunheim to arm himself, and the Jotun helped him by constructing a giant out of clay to fight alongside Hrungnir. The giant was named Mokkurkalfi, and he stood nine leagues tall and three leagues broad at the shoulders, was powered by the heart of a mare, and armed with a stone head and stone weapons. But the heart of the mare trembled when it saw Thor, and they say this clay giant wet himself in fear at Thor's approach.

In his great rage, Thor ignored the clay giant and threw Mjolnir straight at Hrungnir, who threw his whetstone back at Thor. The hammer and stone collided, and the whetstone broke (some stone shrapnel remained lodged in Thor's head, but didn't seem to bother him much), but Mjolnir kept flying straight and hit its mark, shattering Hrungnir's skull. The Jotun fell forward dead and landed across Thor's leg. Meanwhile, Thialfi, who was traveling with Thor, easily killed Mokkurkalfi, but when he tried to lift Hrungnir off Thor's leg, he couldn't, and Thor remained pinned. The other Aesir rushed to Thor's aid, but the only one who could lift the dead Jotun was Thor's three-year-old son named Magni, who apologized for arriving so late and not in time to knock Hrungnir's head off all the way to Hel.

Thor was exceptionally proud of his son for displaying unnatural strength and aggression, and he rewarded him with Gullfaxi, Hrungnir's horse. Odin was a bit salty about this and asked Thor why he'd give such a fine horse to his son birthed by a Jotun woman (apparently not Thor's wife, Sif) when he should have given the horse to his father instead.

Now You Know

Animated beings of clay appear in legends around the world. Mokkurkalfi bears striking resemblance to the golem of Jewish mythology—a being shaped from clay that enacts the commandments of its creator—or the Stallu in Sámi (the Indigenous peoples of northern Fenno-Scandinavia) folklore, which could be conjured by outsiders to terrorize Sámi communities. In other mythologies and religions, humans are shaped from clay, like the god Prometheus molding humans in Greek mythology, fetuses made from the clay of the Nile being deposited in mothers' wombs by the god Khnum in Egyptian mythology, or Allah making the first man out of clay in the Islamic Quran. Maori (New Zealand) cosmology tells us that the forest god Tane Mahuta shaped the first woman out of clay, while the Hindu god Ganesha was born when his mother sculpted a little boy from clay. Whether the beings are benevolent or malevolent, sacred or supernatural, these stories all demonstrate a basic scientific truth: Water and earth are essential ingredients for creating and sustaining life!

ALVIS THE DWARF

ALSO KNOWN AS: **ALVÍSS**

OLD NORSE TRANSLATION: **"ALL-WISE"**

Alvis is one of the only dwarves in Old Norse mythology who has his own story. Despite his name and knowledge in the area of trivia, he proved himself to be rather unwise in strategy and lacking in cunning. While we don't know his backstory or where he came from, we do know that he was not capable of outsmarting even Thor.

THE STORY YOU NEED TO KNOW:

Alvis appears as a main character in the Poetic Edda poem *Alvissmal.* In this story, he visited Thor as a suitor, intent on marrying Thor's daughter and bringing her to live with him in his underground estate. Due to the difference in social status between an Aesir's daughter and a dwarf, Thor was not in a hurry to allow this marriage, and the first thing he did when Alvis approached was insult him, calling him a monster undeserving of any bride, never mind a goddess, and asking if he spent the night with a corpse given his dwarfly pallor. Alvis insulted Thor in return, asking him who he was and how a scoundrel like him could ever be related to, or responsible for, such a beautiful girl as Thor's daughter.

After identities and intentions were established, and a few more insults were hurled, Thor said that he would never grant permission for his daughter to marry Alvis until the dwarf could answer each and every one of the questions that Thor asked him. Thor's questions were a bit vague, comprising various renditions of: What do "they" call different natural phenomena? Alvis gave detailed answers, providing the names for the earth, sky, sun, moon, different types of weather, and geographical features, according to several different species. Humans, Aesir, Vanir, Jotun, elves, and dwarves all had different names for such things, and Alvis, the All-Wise dwarf, he knew them all. Some entities were even called by different names in Hel, and Alvis knew those names too. The names were often descriptive and evocative, and sometimes they indicated whether the phenomena were considered good, bad, indifferent, or useful for specific purposes to creatures throughout the realms. For example, Vanir like Njord felt peaceful and at home by the sea, and their term for the sea, "Restful Harbor," reflected that vibe, while the dwarves described it as "deep, deep sea," evoking an element of mystery (the sea would be unfamiliar territory since dwarves lived in caves underground).

The trivia contest continued, with Thor asking questions and Alvis never missing an answer in all the languages he knew. Clouds were called "Helmets of the Hidden" in Hel, barley was called "Things to Make Beer" by the elves, night was called "Queen of Dreams" by the dwarves, and so on. At this point, we might start to worry about Thor's daughter, because she had not yet spoken (and she never did get a word in) in this test that would decide her fate in marriage, and it seemed like Alvis would be able to correctly answer all Thor's trivia questions. But Thor, who was not usually renowned for cleverness, had figured out how to outsmart this cave-dwelling dwarf. Thor kept asking more and more questions, and Alvis kept giving long-winded answers until Thor finally agreed he had never met a creature that knew so much about so many things!

While duly impressed with the dwarf's knowledge, Thor had deceived him and made him lose all track of time, stalling and keeping him up until dawn. As the sun rose, it began to shine through the windows in Thor's hall, and poof! Alvis the dwarf was turned to stone, caught in the sunlight when he should have returned to his underground home.

NOW YOU KNOW

What's the difference between elves and dwarves in Old Norse myth? Well, the short answer is, there might not be much difference, despite Alvis's differentiating their languages. The difference between elves and dwarves (or "dark elves") might be that the latter tended to live underground. But these supernatural critters might have been ambiguous, imagined differently by everyone, especially since they lack clear descriptions in the primary sources because no one had ever seen an elf or dwarf. What we do know is that they were smaller than humans, usually employed as smiths, and not particularly influential in the grand scheme of the myths. Other than the lists of dwarf names in the poem *Voluspa*, that's about all we know for sure.

GEIRROD, GJALP, AND GREIP

OLD NORSE TRANSLATION: **"PROTECTION FROM SPEARS";
"ROARING ONE"; "GRASP"**
KEY FAMILY MEMBERS: **EACH OTHER**

Geirrod was another belligerent Jotun who appears in *Skaldskaparmal* in the Prose Edda. In another version of this adventure tale that appears in Saxo's *The History of the Danes*, he was King Geruthus of a legendary Scandinavian kingdom. But in either case, he had (at least) two daughters, named Gjalp and Greip. The family crossed paths with Thor and Loki in their adventures, and like most Jotun who tangled with the quick-to-anger Thor and the ever-manipulative Loki, they came to regret their involvement.

THE STORY YOU NEED TO KNOW:

One day, while Loki was borrowing Freyja's falcon feather suit (as he often did), he flew around and saw Geirrod's great hall and courtyard. In his bird form, he dropped down and peeked through the window to get a better look just as Geirrod looked out. Seeing such an unusual and magnificent bird, Geirrod decided that he needed it. He sent a servant out to capture the bird, and Loki taunted him for a while, making him climb all the way to the top of the treacherously high walls to reach him. But when Loki went to fly away at the last minute, he realized his feet were stuck in the wall, and he was captured and brought before the Jotun king.

As he looked more closely at this peculiar bird, Geirrod could see that it had human eyes, not bird eyes, and demanded to know the true identity of the bird. Loki, in falcon form, said nothing. Enraged by the fact that this bird refused to talk, Geirrod locked him in a wooden chest alone for three months, and there Loki starved until Geirrod gave him a second chance to redeem his life.

As usual, especially when he was hungry, Loki bargained for his life with the lives of others. Loki promised Geirrod that if he released him, he would send Thor to Geirrod's halls, but would make sure he had neither his hammer Mjolnir nor his special girdle of might that multiplied his strength. This appealed to Geirrod, as Thor's reputation as a Jotun-killer made him a prime target for revenge, especially if he didn't have his supernatural weapons to defend himself so easily. So, the deal was struck, and Loki went on his way.

Thor, meanwhile, was lodging with a Jotun woman named Grid, who was a bit more agreeable than your average Jotun woman (probably because she was the mother of Vidar, another of Odin's sons and Thor's half-brother, and accustomed to associating with the Aesir). She suspected that Geirrod was up to something and warned Thor of potential mischief, and seeing that he was unarmed, she lent him her own girdle of might, a pair of iron gauntlets, and a staff.

Thor set out to find Geirrod and came to a river called "Vimur," which he had to wade across to reach the Jotun's court. But the water kept rising, making it impassable, and searching for the source, he eventually found it: A Jotun woman was straddling the river, causing it to rise (either via urination or menstrual blood—Snorri is a bit vague on the specifics when it comes to bodily fluids). To punish her for this unsanitary inconvenience, Thor found a giant boulder in the river and hurled it at her, knocking her down. He then waded across, pulled himself up by a rowan tree, and climbed out of the river on the other side.

When Thor finally arrived at Geirrod's court, he was shown to his lodging in the goat shed (other Aesir might have been offended by this, but Thor, of course, really liked goats, so he did not protest). Seeing only one chair, Thor sat down and was comfortable until he realized that his seat was rising too. Geirrod's daughters Gjalp and Greip were lifting his chair, trying to mash him into the ceiling and crush him. Bracing himself against the rafters with the staff he had borrowed from Grid, Thor pushed himself back down, and with a great crack and a snap, the two women let out screams of agony—Thor had broken their backs.

Geirrod then invited Thor into his great hall, alight with many brightly burning fireplaces, under the pretense of playing games. Seeing Thor enter from across the hall, Geirrod welcomed him by grabbing a hot chunk of near-molten iron out of a fireplace with tongs and throwing it at him as hard as he could. Thor caught it with the iron gauntlets from Grid, and Geirrod realized he was in trouble. He hid behind an iron pillar, but Thor took that piece of molten iron and threw it back with such force that it smashed through the pillar and went right through Geirrod's body, as well as the wall behind him, landing on the ground outside.

And that was the end of Geirrod, Gjalp, and Greip, proving that even without Mjolnir, Thor was not one to be trifled with—and Loki was not one to bargain with.

SKRYMIR

ALSO KNOWN AS: UTGARDA-LOKI; UTGARÐALOKI

OLD NORSE TRANSLATION: "BOASTER," "OTHERWORLD LOKI"

Skrymir was a Jotun who Thor and Loki encountered in *Gylfaginning* in the Prose Edda. He went by two names interchangeably, or had two alter egos: Skrymir and Utgarda-Loki. Despite their similar names, Utgarda-Loki was not related to regular Loki—he's not a family member or alternate version. But if we translate the name "Loki" as "Knot-Tangler," the name Utgarda-Loki makes a bit more sense based on their other key similarity: Both were tricksters who liked to mess with Thor.

For Skrymir, the translation of "Jotun" to "giant" is actually fitting. Unlike the other Jotun, who were similar in size to the Aesir, Skrymir was in fact enormous, according to this story, or at least he used magic that made him and his possessions appear deceptively large. He was also unusual in that he seemed to have advanced knowledge of how the universe works, enough to bend the rules of reality, instead of being a dumb brute with tunnel vision like the other Jotun adversaries of Thor and Odin.

THE STORY YOU NEED TO KNOW:

Thor and Loki were out adventuring in Jotunheim, as they often did. One night, they lodged with the farmer Egil. Thor slaughtered his two chariot-pulling goats for dinner and shared his meal with the family—but he cautioned them to be careful with the bones and skins. Egil's son Thialfi didn't listen, and while Thor was asleep, Thialfi broke a leg bone to suck the marrow out. In the morning, Thor took the bones and hides of his goats and brought them back to life with magic from Mjolnir. But one of the poor goats was limping from the broken leg, sending Thor into a fiery rage. Egil gave his son Thialfi and daughter Roskva to Thor as servants to make up for the goat's injury, and Thor made the children carry his knapsack. They continued their adventure over the sea and into a large forest.

When night came and the forest grew dark, Thor, Loki, and the two children searched for lodging and found a massive building with a wide entrance. Thor found himself a nice private room off to the side, and the traveling companions all settled down to sleep—until they were suddenly awoken by an earthquake. They searched for the cause of the rumble with no luck. Thor stood guard in the doorway with Mjolnir, while the other three cowered behind him. In the light of dawn, Thor spied a large sleeping figure in the woods nearby and determined this was the cause of the disturbance. He prepared to whack the sleeping giant with his hammer, but for the first and only time in his life, Thor hesitated out of fear, and the giant awoke, introducing himself as Skrymir. He asked what they were doing in his glove. They realized that the hall they slept in was in fact Skrymir's glove, and the side chamber where Thor slept was for his thumb. Skrymir offered to travel with them, and even carried their food in his knapsack so the children didn't have to.

The next night, Skrymir told them to make supper while he napped, snoring loudly. But they could not untie the knot in the knapsack, much to the hungry frustration of Thor. He whacked Skrymir in the head with Mjolnir as hard as he could. The giant awakened, and asked if a leaf had just fallen on him—he wasn't the slightest bit injured. The following morning, Skrymir departed from their company but gave them directions to Utgard Castle. Upon arriving, Thor tried to open the gates, but he was not strong enough. The group then realized that they could squeeze through the bars of the gate to get in.

Once inside, they found the king of the hall, Utgarda-Loki. He had the audacity to call Thor small, and told them they were only welcome to stay if they performed some superior feat. Loki announced that his remarkable skill was eating faster than anyone, and so Utgarda-Loki challenged him to an eating contest against his servant Logi, which Loki lost. Thialfi claimed he could run faster than anyone, but was defeated in a race by Utgarda-Loki's servant named Hugi. Utgarda-Loki then demanded to know what accomplishments Thor could demonstrate. Thor played to his strengths and challenged Utgarda-Loki to a drinking contest. He was brought a great drinking horn and took a big gulp—but the level was unchanged. Thor gulped and gulped, but he didn't make a dent in the beer. He kept trying, while Utgarda-Loki laughed and insulted him and finally offered him an alternative: He wanted to see if tiny Thor could lift his giant cat.

Thor was angered by the insults and his own failure, and so he tried to lift the cat but couldn't. He only succeeded in raising a single paw. Utgarda-Loki offered him another alternative: He wanted to see if Thor could defeat his old maid Elli in a wrestling contest. Thor again accepted the challenge, but it was not long before the old woman defeated him, with Thor falling to one knee. At this point, Utgarda-Loki told Thor there was no point in challenging him any further but nonetheless offered the four travelers his hospitality.

Thor had never been so humiliated until Utgarda-Loki explained exactly how they were defeated: Skrymir's knapsack was fastened with trick wire (here Utgarda-Loki confessed to being Skrymir too). When Thor tried to whack him in the head but Skrymir felt nothing, it was because he had moved a mountain between the hammer and his head when Thor wasn't looking, and Thor's blows were enough to create valleys. Logi was able to outeat Loki because he was in fact an all-consuming wildfire disguised as a man, and Hugi was an embodiment of Utgarda-Loki's thought, and there was no way the boy could outrun a thought. The drinking horn that Thor couldn't drain was funneled from the ocean, and Thor drank so much the tide went out, but Thor was so frustrated he didn't notice. Utgarda-Loki's giant cat was in fact the Midgard Serpent, and it was miraculous that Thor could lift even a paw—if he had lifted much more, he could have damaged the whole world the serpent was wrapped around. And no one would be able to defeat Elli in combat since the elderly maid was in fact old age itself.

Angered that he had been tricked so many times, Thor lifted his hammer to start smashing again, but in the blink of an eye, Utgarda-Loki and his whole castle disappeared, leaving Thor and his companions looking out across a vast, empty landscape, thoroughly thwarted and bamboozled.

HARBARTH

ALSO KNOWN AS: **HARBARÐ**

OLD NORSE TRANSLATION: **"GREYBEARD"**

KEY FAMILY MEMBERS: **SEE ODIN'S FAMILY RELATIONS IN PART 2**

The name "Greybeard" evokes Odin's go-to disguise: an old man with a long grey beard, leaning on a staff and wearing a long cloak. Enigmatic and mysterious, Odin-as-Greybeard might appear to a soldier on a battlefield moments before death or as a wanderer arriving unexpectedly at a key moment to give advice and help a hero make a fortunate decision. However, humans were not the only beings who had chance encounters with Greybeard; he could appear in far more mundane circumstances as well. In the poem *Harbarthsljoth* in the Poetic Edda, Odin is a main character but identifies himself by the pseudonym "Greybeard" and appears as a ferryman who does not feel like being particularly helpful to a weary traveler—who happens to be Thor.

The argument between father and son seemed to occur for no reason in particular. Maybe Odin was just having a bad day and knew Thor would be an easy target to get a rise out of. The banter between them turned into a fierce competition of *drengskapr*, or Norse masculinity ideals, and despite Odin's disguised appearance, his clues and false name were so obvious that Thor most likely knew exactly who he was dealing with. But any challenge or insult to one's masculinity had to be avenged, no matter who issued it.

THE STORY YOU NEED TO KNOW:

Thor was walking back to Asgard after a long journey when his path led him to a fjord. On the other side of the water, he could see a ferryman sitting next to a boat, and he called out for a ride across. Thor asked the ferryman to tell him his name, and Thor offered him food in exchange for passage across the fjord, since Thor had already enjoyed a large breakfast of herring and goat and was not yet hungry for lunch. The ferryman refused Thor's bargain and denied him passage, taunting him instead. He scolded Thor for boasting about his breakfast, implied that his mother would be dead by the time he got home, and—if that's not bad enough—said his pants were stupid-looking. After hearing these insults, Thor identified himself as the great warrior of the gods and son of Odin, hoping to frighten some manners into this insolent ferryman, and again asked for his name. The ferryman responded that he rarely lied about his name (obviously not true) and after some bantering finally told Thor his name was Greybeard.

Because Thor was reluctant to get his pants wet, and Greybeard refused to row over and give him a ride, the two hurled insults across the water, boasting of their respective accomplishments and asking the other what they had been doing recently. Greybeard told Thor that he would be his fiercest enemy since Hrungnir, but Thor responded that he killed Hrungnir easily—and what had Greybeard been doing, anyway? Greybeard

bragged about waging a five-year war on the island of Algron, killing countless warriors, and then seducing and raping several women, stealing them from their husbands—and what had Thor been up to? He killed Thiassi (the Jotun who kidnapped Ithunn) and several other Jotun women of the mountains (like Gjalp and Greip), for those evil Jotun would have murdered every human in Midgard had they survived—and what else had Greybeard done? Greybeard pitted princes against each other, stirred up battle and death so that Odin might receive the glorious fallen and Thor could have their lowly servants. And what had Thor done lately? Greybeard heard he got stepped on like an itty-bitty coward while sleeping in a giant's glove (a reference to his encounter with Skrymir).

At this point, Thor must surely have been aware that Greybeard was Odin, but for whatever reason, he seemed equal parts outraged by his father's insults and content to play along with Odin's disguise. Thor called Greybeard a pansy and threatened to kill him when he made it across the fjord—but the ferryman reminded him that this was hardly a legitimate threat, seeing as he was clearly incapable of wading across the fjord. Greybeard continued to gloat about his graphic battles and sexual conquests, while Thor listed more of his slain adversaries. Greybeard (ironically) shamed Thor for battling against women, but Thor insisted that they were monsters, not real women—and Thor assured him he would have helped Greybeard hold down some of his beautiful, unwilling victims, had the opportunity presented itself.

Eventually, they grew tired of slandering each other, and so Greybeard told Thor to go home and maybe he'd get there in time to catch his wife's lover. Thor accused him of lying about his wife's affair but nonetheless asked for directions to get around the fjord since the ferryman wouldn't help him across. Greybeard told Thor how to reach Midgard, where his mother, Jord, could give him directions to Asgard (the classic "go ask your mother"). Get out of here, said Greybeard—go home, and have a horrible rest of your day.

NOW YOU KNOW

The victimization of women was common in Norse literature, and while this was a brutal fact of life for Viking-era women, there are also several examples that glorify strong, independent women. One particularly strong example is from one of the sagas telling the history of the Icelanders, called *The Saga of the People of Laxdale*. In it, a woman named Aud suffers a humiliating divorce after her husband's mistress convinces him to accuse her of wearing pants (wearing clothes of the opposite gender was legal grounds for divorce). Aud gets her revenge by putting on pants, riding out in the middle of the night, breaking into his new house while he and his new wife (the mistress) are asleep, slicing him across the chest, stabbing him in the arm, and making him faint from blood loss. Aud's brothers are quite proud of her, but tell her she should have injured him worse.

PART 4

HUMAN HEROES

Famous human heroes were idolized and recorded in the legendary sagas of Norse myth (the ones I'm referencing here are *The Saga of the Volsungs*, *The Saga of Ragnar Lothbrok*, *The Saga of Hrolf Kraki and His Champions*, *The Saga of Hervor and Heidrek*, and *The Saga of Egil One-Hand and Asmund Berserkers-Slayer*). Legendary sagas tell the stories of mostly fictional royal or aristocratic families, from father and mother to sons and daughters across generations. The stories build chronologically through the lineage (so for this part, it would definitely be helpful to read the character entries in order). Some of these names may loosely reference real people, but the characters are fantastically embellished beyond recognizable historical truth, and the stories surrounding them involve all sorts of supernatural elements. They are Vikings and kings and shield-maidens and queens, who interact with gods, marry Valkyries, slay dragons, conquer great enemies against unbeatable odds, and face death with courage and nerves of steel.

But that's not to say that our heroes are perfect or ideal humans—in fact, they often make bloody mistakes and rash decisions. On one hand, the men may act out of anger, pride, or greed, and decide not to listen to their female relatives who give warnings about the potentially fatal consequences of their actions. Seidh, or prophecy, is often associated with goddesses, and that skill may trickle down to the human world as well. These human women may have intuition or premonitions that the men in their lives do not, but that doesn't mean their advice will be heeded. On the other hand, women may find themselves caught between a rock and a hard place, with their loyalties torn between their birth families and their married families (and to make matters more complicated, they might even have grievances against both sides), and in this unfortunate position and male-dominated society, women may exercise what little power they have and make some choices that they ultimately regret.

VOLSUNG

ALSO KNOWN AS: VÖLSUNG, VǪLSUNG
OLD NORSE TRANSLATION: ROUGHLY "VIRILE"
KEY FAMILY MEMBERS: SON SIGMUND; DAUGHTER SIGNY

Volsung is the first main character in the epic legendary saga *The Saga of the Volsungs*. While his forefathers were a bit misfortunate, many of his descendants were famous heroes, including Sigurd and Helgi, and the line was imbued with further renown and glory when the legendary Ragnar Lothbrok married into the family. Characters and episodes from *The Saga of the Volsungs* are retold and alluded to in many poems throughout the Poetic Edda as well, particularly those involving Helgi and Sigurd (and the women Sigurd became entangled with, Brynhild and Gudrun), but the saga itself tells the most coherent version of events regarding the members of this family.

THE STORY YOU NEED TO KNOW:

Once upon a time, there was a man named Sigi, who was a mortal son of Odin. Sigi was wealthy and powerful and involved in a bit of a "keeping up with the Joneses" competition with another man named Skadi. On a hunting trip, Sigi was upset that Skadi's enslaved person Bredi killed more animals than him, and so he murdered him to avoid being humiliated by an enslaved person. Bredi's body was later found in a snowbank, and Sigi was banished and outlawed from the kingdom as punishment for committing the unjustified murder.

But his father, Odin, helped him, providing him with a warship and Viking crew, whom Sigi led on to many victorious battles and raids, once again amassing wealth and restoring his good name. He became the king of a new kingdom and produced a son named Rerir, who grew to be strong and accomplished like his father.

But as Sigi grew older, he was ambushed and betrayed by his brothers-in-law, who murdered him and his bodyguards. Rerir heard of this and summoned all his friends into a great army, and proclaimed his kinship with his uncles invalid after such a dishonorable betrayal. He killed all his uncles and absorbed their kingdoms into that of his father, and he became an even greater king than his father before him.

Rerir married his queen and loved her very much, and for years they tried to produce a child with no luck. They prayed to the gods for assistance, and Frigg answered their prayer. Frigg told Odin to intervene, and so Odin gave a Valkyrie named Hljod a magic apple to deliver to Rerir. She transformed herself into a crow and dropped it in his lap. He ate the apple and then went to his wife, and soon thereafter she became pregnant.

While this should have been a happy time for Rerir and his queen, what followed was a tragedy. Rerir went out to battle, but instead of dying honorably, he contracted and succumbed to an illness. Meanwhile, the queen was unable to give birth. She remained pregnant for six years until she could simply stand it no longer and demanded to be cut open, knowing she couldn't survive much longer either way. The child was revealed to be a boy of about six years old. He kissed his mother as she lay dying, and he was named Volsung, and he inherited the throne from his father. Volsung also became a great man and victorious warrior, eventually marrying Hljod, the same Valkyrie who had brought his father the magic apple. They had a happy marriage, producing ten sons and one daughter. The oldest and fairest of the children were twins, his son Sigmund and daughter Signy.

Another king, named Siggeir, desired to marry Signy. While she did not return his affection, their union would be politically strategic, and so King Volsung insisted she marry him despite her distrust and disapproval. Volsung had built a magnificent hall around a large oak tree called "Barnstokk," with the trunk in the middle of the hall and its branches and blossoms stretching upward into the rafters, and this hall was where the wedding feast was held. An uninvited guest came into the hall during the feast—an elderly man who wore a long cloak and wide-brimmed hat (you guessed it, Odin). He pulled out a sword and stabbed it deep into the tree trunk, announcing that anyone who could pull the sword free would be entitled to keep it, and no better sword would ever be found. All the highborn men tried to claim it, but only Sigmund, Volsung's son, was able to remove it.

King Siggeir was jealous and angry at having been bested at his own wedding feast, and he offered to buy it from Sigmund for the price of the sword's weight in gold. But Sigmund refused, saying that he could never sell such a fine sword that was clearly meant for him. Siggeir felt mocked and humiliated by this reply but decided to act dismissive and pretended to go back to enjoying Volsung's feast. That night, after the festivities were concluded, he took his bride to bed and started to think up an appropriate revenge against the Volsung family for denying him this fabulous sword.

NOW YOU KNOW

The suffix "-ung" usually denotes a family, therefore making the character Volsung indistinguishable from the family he begot. However, it's quite likely that his original name was Volsi, and the legendary stature of his offspring (Vols-ung) and his role as the main patriarch led to his being linguistically conflated with the whole family. But the name "Volsi" is also unusual and rare, meaning "phallus of a stallion," most likely a reference to the virility of stallions. The name is not altogether surprising, given that he produced eleven children, an impressive feat considering his father's difficulty by comparison. The name of his hall, "Barnstokk," however, is not at all unusual. "Barn" still means "child" in the modern Nordic languages (Swedish, Norwegian, Danish), and "stokk" is the Old Norse word for "tree trunk," and as such Volsung has literally constructed the "family tree"—the site of this almost Arthurian sword-pulling episode.

SIGNY

ALSO KNOWN AS: **SIGNÝ, SIGNE**
OLD NORSE TRANSLATION: **"NEW VICTORY"**
KEY FAMILY MEMBERS: BROTHER **SIGMUND;**
HUSBAND SIGGEIR; SON SINFJOLTI

Signy was King Volsung's only daughter, twin sister to Sigmund, and older sister to the other nine Volsung brothers. She was pretty tough, as you might expect since she grew up around that many boys. But because she was married to King Siggeir against her better judgment, she was also desperately unhappy. Perhaps it was fate over free will, or perhaps it was drengr stubbornness (remember, "drengr" essentially means "macho," "badass," and "brute"), but Signy glimpsed the future and knew it was dire— yet her pleas were futile, as none of the men in her life would listen to her warnings.

THE STORY YOU NEED TO KNOW:

The morning after the wedding feast of Signy and Siggeir, Siggeir told King Volsung that he wanted to depart for home as soon as possible, while the seas were calm and the weather was good. Later, Signy also went to her father and begged him not to let Siggeir take her away with him. Volsung scolded her, reminding her how scandalous it would be to break this marriage contract when Siggeir had committed no offense. The family would lose their good name and become distrusted in all their friendships and alliances. But Signy in turn reminded him that she was gifted with second sight, like many of the women of their family before her, and she warned him of impending disaster if he didn't change his mind. But Volsung held fast, and as Siggeir prepared to leave, he apologized for leaving so soon and invited his new in-laws to join him for a feast at his home to make up for his hasty departure.

Volsung and his sons agreed to visit Siggeir and Signy, unaware that Siggeir was plotting revenge against Volsung and his family for not selling him the sword that Sigmund pulled from the tree trunk. The evening they arrived, Signy snuck onto their boats before they came ashore and told them that Siggeir was planning to betray them. She begged her father to turn around and take her home with them, and not fall into her wicked husband's trap. But Volsung reminded his daughter that when he was still in his mother's womb, he swore an oath never to flee from iron nor fire, and even as an old man he would not be a coward. He also yelled at her for doubting her brothers, who were just as brave and valiant and would likewise never fear death nor run from a fight. Volsung told her to go back to her husband and stay with him regardless of what happened to them.

The next morning, Volsung and his sons, accompanied only by their small contingent of men, prepared themselves for battle. They disembarked from their boats, but before they reached Siggeir's hall, he greeted them with a massive army. Volsung and his sons cut through the ranks of Siggeir's army eight times over, fighting with weapons in both hands, but on the ninth assault,

Volsung fell dead in the middle of the battle. After his fall, his greatly outnumbered men were killed by Siggeir's army, except for his ten sons, who were captured and brought back to Siggeir's hall.

When Signy learned that her father was dead and her brothers had been captured, and all the tragedy that she had feared had come true, she made a single request of her husband: Instead of beheading her brothers immediately, would he consider holding them in the stocks for a while? She expected that this was too much to hope for from him. Siggeir laughed at her and called her foolish, but he agreed to honor her request only because he enjoyed the idea of the brothers suffering longer before they died. A large tree trunk was laid down across their legs, pinning the brothers to the ground.

As night fell, a hideous wolf (said to be Siggeir's mother using witchcraft) found the brothers in this predicament, and she tore one man apart with her teeth and devoured him. In the morning, when Signy sent a servant to check on them, she learned of her brother's fate. She was horrified to learn the consequences of her attempt to save them. Night after night, the wolf returned and ate another brother, until the tenth night, when only Sigmund was left. But Signy had an idea—she gave her servant honey and instructed him to smear it all over Sigmund's face and put some in his mouth. When the wolf came to devour Sigmund, she noticed the honey and started licking it off his face first, and then stuck her tongue into his mouth to get the remaining honey. Sigmund then bit down on the wolf's tongue, and the wolf sprang back and struggled against him, but still Sigmund held on with his teeth so hard that the wolf ripped her tongue out of her own throat and then died from the injury.

In the struggle, the stocks that had held Sigmund down were destroyed, and when a messenger told Signy the news, she was overjoyed to have saved at least one brother. They met in secret and decided that he should build a house deep in the woods and stay until they could avenge their father and brothers. She smuggled supplies to him for a decade, successfully keeping him hidden, all the while letting Siggeir think that all the Volsungs were dead. As the years passed, Siggeir and Signy had two sons together, and Siggeir thought that he had defeated the mighty Volsungs.

SIGMUND

ALSO KNOWN AS: **SIGEMUND**

OLD NORSE TRANSLATION: **"VICTORY," "PROTECTOR"**

KEY FAMILY MEMBERS: **SISTER SIGNY; SONS SINFJOLTI,
SIGURD, AND HELGI**

As the last surviving Volsung man, Sigmund was now responsible for carrying on the family line, and honor demanded that he avenge his family by killing his brother-in-law, Siggeir. Signy was determined to help her brother kill her husband (whom she thoroughly despised), though her methods may seem a bit extreme by today's standards.

THE STORY YOU NEED TO KNOW:

While Sigmund lived in his secret cabin in the woods, Signy gave birth to two sons. When the oldest was about ten years old, she sent him out into the woods to meet his uncle Sigmund, hoping that the boy would help achieve Volsung revenge against Siggeir. Sigmund gave the boy a sack of flour, told him to bake bread, and meanwhile went out to collect some firewood. But when he came back, the boy had done absolutely nothing—he was afraid to touch the flour since he was convinced there was something alive in the sack. When Sigmund told Signy her son was a coward, she responded that he might as well kill the boy if he was useless, so Sigmund did so. Two years later, Signy sent her younger son to Sigmund, but this meeting went much the same, and Signy instructed Sigmund to kill him too.

Queen Signy by chance met a powerful witch, and she decided that they should change forms. The witch agreed and slept next to King Siggeir, who was none the wiser, while Signy went to visit her brother. She told him she was lost in the woods and wished to spend the night. Not recognizing his sister as the witch, he offered her his hospitality and noticed that she was very beautiful. After dinner, he asked if she would like to share his bed, and she didn't refuse—they slept together for the next three nights. Signy then went home to find the witch, and they returned to their original appearances.

Nine months later, Signy gave birth to a boy named Sinfjolti. He grew strong and handsome, and before his tenth birthday, Signy decided to test his courage. She sewed his sleeves onto his arms, and then ripped them off, taking the skin with them. But Sinfjolti did not complain, as did her previous sons. Signy sent Sinfjolti to Sigmund, who tested him similarly. Instead of being afraid, Sinfjolti kneaded down the creature in the flour bag. When Sigmund saw this, he laughed and told the boy not to eat the bread—he'd succeeded in grinding and baking a poisonous snake. Sinfjolti was not like Signy's other sons, and so Sigmund began training him, getting him accustomed to battle and hardship. In their adventures, they found some wolf skins and decided to wear them, but they became stuck. The two men became wolves, their voices turned to howls, and they killed all the men they came across. On the tenth day, Sigmund and

Sinfjolti returned to the cabin and were finally able to remove the wolf skins, and they burned them so that no one would ever get stuck as a wolf again.

In the years that passed, Signy continued to live unhappily with Siggeir, and they had a couple more children together, but she didn't like them any more than their previous children who she had murdered. When the time was ripe, Signy, Sigmund, and Sinfjolti planned their vengeance against Siggeir. As they hid in the darkness, one of Signy's new sons with Siggeir saw them and told his father about two grim men infiltrating the hall. Signy heard her son betray them, and she told Sigmund to kill the child. Sigmund insisted he didn't want to kill any more of her children, but Sinfjolti stepped in and murdered him without hesitation.

The damage had already been done, though, and Siggeir's army was ready for Sigmund and Sinfjolti. Though they fought bravely and skillfully, they were outnumbered, and having lost the element of surprise, they were captured. Siggeir decided to tie them both on separate sides of a massive rock and then bury them alive so that they could hear each other suffer but neither see nor help each other. As Siggeir's enslaved people filled in the hole, Signy secretly tossed in an armful of straw, and lucky for Sigmund and Sinfjolti, the straw was wrapped around a side of bacon and Sigmund's sword.

Sigmund and Sinfjolti cut through earth and stone to escape and set fire to Siggeir's hall that night. Siggeir, in his confusion, asked what had happened, and Sigmund introduced himself and informed Siggeir that not all the Volsungs were dead. Sigmund called for his sister, hoping to compensate her for her misery now that they were victorious, but she arrived looking unhappy. She told her husband of the great lengths she had gone to, killing their children and plotting against him. She then told her brother about the witch and her deception, and she told Sinfjolti that his greatness was a result of both his parents being Volsungs. And as payment for these sins, Signy felt she deserved death and elected to burn alongside Siggeir.

Sigmund and Sinfjolti went on many Viking raids together and reclaimed the ancestral kingdom of the Volsungs. Sigmund married Borghild, and they had two sons named Helgi and Hamund. Helgi and Sinfjolti also traveled together, accomplishing great deeds. But Sinfjolti later killed Borghild's brother in a fight over a woman, and Borghild poisoned Sinfjolti, killing him. Sigmund nearly died from grief over losing his nephew-son and divorced and banished Borghild.

Sigmund later remarried a beautiful and wise woman named Hjordis, who was also courted by King Lyngvi. Angered because Hjordis chose Sigmund, Lyngvi traveled to Sigmund's kingdom after their wedding and attacked. Though aging in years, Sigmund fought like a true Volsung hero, protecting his wife and home—until a mysterious man on the battlefield appeared in a cloak and slayed him (yup, Odin again—to claim Sigmund for his own Ragnarok army, of course!).

Hjordis hid from Lyngvi and managed to escape, and she later found her dying husband on the battlefield. Sigmund told her that he was injured beyond hope but not to despair, for they would be avenged. He told her that she was pregnant with a son, who would be so great a warrior that he would never be forgotten. Sigmund entrusted to Hjordis the broken fragments of his sword and told her to save it for their son when he was ready to claim it.

HELGI

OLD NORSE TRANSLATION: "HAPPY"

KEY FAMILY MEMBERS: FATHER SIGMUND; WIFE SVAVA/SIGRUN

Helgi is usually described as the son of Sigmund and his first wife, Borghild. He was the half-brother to Sinfjolti (son of Sigmund and Signy) and Sigurd (son of Sigmund and Hjordis). While Sigurd is the brother in this generation who primarily carries on *The Saga of the Volsungs*, Helgi was also a prominent warrior worthy of the Volsung bloodline, and he is featured in three poems in the Poetic Edda as well: *Helgakvitha Hjorvarthssonar* and *Helgakvitha Hundingsbana I* and *II*. He is best known for his extraordinary successes in battle, which resulted in his marriage to a beautiful Valkyrie (or princess). However, because many of the stories feature key variations (for example, was his wife's name Svava or Sigrun?), the medieval manuscript editors decided they'd explain away the gnawing inconsistencies in Helgi's story by introducing a new twist to the Old Norse legends: reincarnation. Helgi and his true love were consistently reincarnated after valiant deeds, destined to be together in this life and the next (and the next...).

THE STORY YOU NEED TO KNOW:

Helgi's story is a bit of a "choose your own adventure" exercise. Was he the son of Sigmund and Borghild, as described in *The Saga of the Volsungs* and the *Helgakvitha Hundingsbana* set of poems from the Poetic Edda? Or was he the son of King Hjorvarth—as told in *Helgakvitha Hjorvarthssonar*—who, after many attempts, finally succeeded in marrying Sigerlinn, the most beautiful woman and daughter of King Svafnir, and produced an heir with her? With either parentage, Helgi grew to be strong, courageous, and handsome.

Let's take the more common variant first: Helgi was Sigmund's son. From the day he was born, the Norns and ravens foretold he would be a great warrior, and Sigmund made him a wealthy prince. By the age of fifteen, he had his own army of noble Vikings, and Helgi led his company in a bloody war against King Hunding. Helgi killed the king and claimed his land, and when Hunding's sons asked him for compensation, he denied them—instead wiping out the whole family.

Helgi captured the attention of the Valkyries, and one named Sigrun, daughter of Hogni, was duly impressed by his prowess in battle and came to Helgi with an offer: Her father had promised her hand in marriage to a man named Hothbrodd, son of Granmar, but Sigrun thought he was grim and unworthy, and she did not want to marry him. So, she invited Helgi to either take her from her father by force or else challenge her betrothed to mortal combat so that she might marry Helgi instead. (In *The Saga of the Volsungs*, she was a princess hiding from the battle in the woods, not a Valkyrie.)

Be she princess or Valkyrie, Helgi accepted her proposal and set out to kill Hothbrodd. He rallied his men and fleet of ships, and Valkyrie Sigrun flew above, protecting them. Upon arriving at Granmar's kingdom, a messenger named Guthmund demanded to know their identity, and Helgi's half-brother Sinfjolti responded, describing Helgi's nobility and threatening death against any who opposed him. The two men engaged in insults until Helgi interrupted, demanding they exchange swords instead of words, and made sure that Odin's wolves and ravens were well-fed. Helgi was victorious and won both his lovely bride and the lands of his fallen foe.

Helgakvitha Hundingsbana II continues this tale, saying that Helgi spared Dag, one of Sigrun's brothers. But Dag was honor-bound to avenge his murdered father and borrowed a special spear from Odin. Only with this cursed spear did Helgi fall, and he was then sent to Valhalla, though he was reborn and met Sigrun in his burial mound to spend one more night with her. She continued to wait for him and then died from her grief when he did not return again.

The other version of this story starts with Helgi's birth as the son of King Hjorvarth. His parents could not think of a name for their son, as he was remarkably strong, handsome, and silent, so it seemed to them that no name could suit him. But one day, a group of Valkyries rode past and one approached him, calling him "Helgi" and prophesizing that he would be a great warrior and ruler. Helgi asked this beautiful woman if she had just given him a name, and if so, what his traditional naming gift might be. He said he would not accept the name unless she was the gift that accompanied it.

Helgi went out on raids to prove himself, and then asked King Eylimi's permission to marry his daughter Svava, the Valkyrie who had named him. They were married and loved each other faithfully. All was blissful until Helgi's half-brother Hethin got drunk and boasted that he would take his brother's wife from him. Hethin later regretted making such a rash oath. Shortly thereafter, Helgi was mortally wounded in battle, and a messenger sent for Svava so that she could see him before he died. Helgi asked Svava to marry his brother Hethin after he died, to spare him the dishonor of breaking his oath, but Svava refused, saying she would love no man but Helgi. He died in her arms, and Hethin kissed Svava and promised to avenge Helgi, the greatest man who had ever lived, and Helgi and Svava were reincarnated.

NOW YOU KNOW

In Norse mythology, the concept of reincarnation—in which a man returns to relive his life and to (re)fulfill his destiny—is most likely inspired by Scandinavia's conversion to Christianity and simply for the sake of convenience. Since these myths were written by a later generation of Christian converts, Helgi's Christ-like rebirth (with his Valkyrie being almost Marian in her ascension due to her devout loyalty to him), might serve a dual purpose: to save the trouble of picking and choosing between story variants, and to make their pagan ancestors a bit more relatable by interweaving current sensibilities with beliefs of the past.

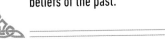

SIGURD

ALSO KNOWN AS: SIGURÐ, SIGURTH, SIGURD THE DRAGON SLAYER

OLD NORSE TRANSLATION: "VICTORY," "GUARDIAN"

KEY FAMILY MEMBERS: FATHER SIGMUND;

WIFE GUDRUN; DAUGHTER ASLAUG

Sigurd was the son of Sigmund and Hjordis, and he became the most famous Volsung warrior and hero. Nicknamed Sigurd the Dragon Slayer, from birth he was unmatched in spirit and boldness, but he became embroiled in a tragic love triangle (actually, it was a love quadrilateral) that would ultimately lead to his demise. He's also a great example of the Norse "fate over free will" idiom, as his uncle Gripir foretold his whole life story, both the accomplishments and the tragedies, in the Poetic Edda poem *Gripisspa*. Nevertheless, Sigurd accepted his fate and lived out his destiny without trying to change it (either that, or he entirely forgot all that he was told). Sigurd's story is intertwined with the next few characters (Brynhild, Gunnar, and Gudrun), so we'll keep adding pieces to their story as we introduce the characters one by one.

THE STORY YOU NEED TO KNOW:

Sigurd's story is told in *The Saga of the Volsungs*, as well as throughout several poems in the Poetic Edda: *Gripisspa*, *Fafnismal*, and *Sigurtharkvitha en skamma*. After the death of his father, Sigmund, his mother, Hjordis, became the wife of King Alf, and Sigurd was raised and educated by a foster father named Regin.

Sigurd was content with his childhood in King Alf's kingdom, but Regin began to needle at him regarding his inheritance and wealth, and he suggested that King Alf shouldn't be trusted with Sigurd's late father's fortune. To prove that his stepfather was honorable, Sigurd asked King Alf for a horse, and Alf granted it freely—whichever horse he chose would be his. As Sigurd was leaving to pick out his horse, he encountered a strange old man with a long grey beard and cloak (Odin, of course!), who offered to help him select the best horse. They together decided on Grani, a descendant of Sleipnir, as noble and great a horse as any mortal could ask for.

Regin continued to taunt young Sigurd, claiming he didn't have enough wealth or courage to be worthy of the Volsung bloodline unless he sought out the greatest, fiercest, largest, wealthiest dragon of all: Regin's brother Fafnir, the dragon who had killed his (human) father Hreidmar for the gold that Odin and Loki had paid him as recompense for killing Hreidmar's other son, Otter (yes, an actual otter). Regin insisted that Sigurd must kill Fafnir and take this treasure for himself, and being young and brave, Sigurd decided to do so; but first, he needed a sword. After Regin made him a few swords that were easily shattered and unfit for dragon-slaying, Sigurd went to his mother and asked about his father's sword, Gram, which was broken on the bat-tlefield when Sigmund was slain (see the Sigmund entry in this part for that story). Sigurd asked Regin to reforge this sword, and when made whole again, Gram became unbreakable. After he went on a Viking raid and killed King Lyngvi to avenge the death of his father, Sigurd set out to find Fafnir.

Sigurd and Regin found the cliff and waterhole where Fafnir lived, and Regin told Sigurd to dig a pit and hide in it and, when the dragon slithered by, stab him in the heart. Regin then fled in terror as Sigurd started digging, but an old man with a grey beard approached and asked Sigurd what he was doing. As Sig-urd explained his plan, the old man (yes, Odin again) told him to dig several holes so that they would all fill with the dragon's blood, instead of just the one hole, which might drown him. Sig-urd took this good advice and waited for Fafnir.

The dragon approached, spitting poison and shaking the earth with his massive size. Sigurd sat bravely in his pit and waited, and then he stabbed Fafnir in the heart and leapt from the ground to face his fallen enemy. With his dying breaths, Fafnir inquired who Sigurd was, and they engaged in a trivia contest about the Volsung family genealogy, the Norns, Ragnarok, and the future. Fafnir predicted that anyone who would take his gold would die because of it, since it was cursed by Loki, just as Fafnir himself was dying by Sigurd's hand over the gold.

Regin then tried to share the credit with Sigurd for killing the dragon, and they decided to cook and eat the dragon's heart. When Sigurd tasted a bit of Fafnir's blood, he was suddenly gifted with the ability to understand the language of birds. Coinciden-tally, several birds in the trees above him were discussing how wise it would be for Sigurd to kill Regin, since Regin was planning to betray him. Taking their advice, Sigurd took Gram and cut off Regin's head. He kept eavesdropping on the birds, who then started talking about the wisdom he might gain if he rode to find Odin's unfaithful Valkyrie who lay sleeping at Hindarfjall.

NOW YOU KNOW

"Gram" means "wrath," a fitting name for the sword Gram, which was broken and reforged, becoming unbreakable. When Regin was reforging Sigmund's sword for Sigurd, it is said that the blade itself looked as though it were aflame. Sounds a bit like Anduril, "the Flame of the West," Aragorn's inherited, broken, and reforged sword in Tolkien's The Lord of the Rings, which may not be unbreakable but does help him fulfill his destiny of uniting the world of men (and allies of other species), defeating the evil Sauron, and reclaiming the throne of Gondor. Tolkien's allusions to Sigurd appear in *The Hobbit*, too, when unlikely hero Bilbo Baggins engages in a trivia and riddle contest with the dragon Smaug.

BRYNHILD

ALSO KNOWN AS: **BRUNHILD, BRYNHILDA**
OLD NORSE TRANSLATION: **LOOSELY "ARMED WOMAN"**
KEY FAMILY MEMBERS: **HUSBAND GUNNAR; BROTHER ATLI; DAUGHTER ASLAUG**

The Valkyrie in Hindarfjall that the birds spoke of was Brynhild, the beautiful daughter of the brave king Buthli, and the shield-maiden who defied Odin's will on the battlefield. She was punished for this transgression with unnatural sleep, and Odin cursed her into eventual marriage so that she could never again alter victories on the battlefield: Brynhild was a warrior woman doomed to become a housewife. Echoing our story about the Valkyrie Sigrdrifa in *Sigrdrifumal*, Brynhild's encounter with Sigurd is described in *The Saga of the Volsungs* and the Poetic Edda's *Gripisspa*. These two names, Brynhild ("Armed Woman") and Sigrdrifa ("Victory Driver") are used interchangeably, and likely they are the same character who sometimes uses a nickname.

THE STORY YOU NEED TO KNOW:

Sigurd rode to Hindarfjall and saw a fortress alight with fire, and inside this ring of fire was a person sleeping in armor. He removed her helmet and armor, and the sleeping woman awoke

and asked who he was and why he had come. He affirmed that he was Sigurd, he had killed Fafnir and acquired his gold, and he was told that he should seek her out, for he heard that she was unmatched in beauty and wisdom. She brought him a drink and told him of her punishment by Odin: that she was stung with a sleep thorn for giving a victory to Agnar instead of Odin's favored king, Hjalm-Gunnar. She mourned that she would never know victory in battle again and instead would be forced to marry.

In response to Odin's punishment, however, she swore an oath to marry only a man without fear. It appeared to Brynhild that man she had sworn to marry might in fact be Sigurd, and perhaps that part of her punishment was not so bad. For Sigurd was well-known to be the bravest of all men, strong and tall, with a handsome face, long brown hair, and a well-groomed beard. In fact, maybe it was no punishment at all.

Brynhild taught Sigurd the wisdom of the runes and gave him other advice, much like Sigrdrifa's advice in *Sigrdrifumal*, the Valkyrie story. She reminded him to be honorable and brave and not to tangle with foolish men, and she also warned him that he could expect to be hated by his brothers-in-law. As they spoke, Sigurd realized that there was no woman in the world who could possibly be as wise as Brynhild, and she was equally taken with him. For she was just as wise and lovely as the birds had told him she would be, and he was fearless, clever, and handsome. Brynhild told Sigurd that if she could choose a husband from all the men in the world, it would be him. And so they agreed to marry, and after spending a few nights together, Sigurd rode off to claim his Volsung-family kingship with the intention of returning to her.

Awoken from her sleep, Brynhild returned to the home of her foster father, Heimir. Her visit was well-timed, as Sigurd was also passing through. When he seemed sad sitting in Heimir's halls and not enjoying the parties and feasts held in his honor, a man named Alsvid asked Sigurd why he could not be happy. Sigurd told him of the remarkable woman he had met, and Alsvid recognized from his descriptions that the woman must be Brynhild. Alsvid told him that Heimir's foster daughter had just come home, about the same time Sigurd had stopped by, and that he might go visit her upstairs—but he also warned him that she had no interest in hospitality and might not receive him, for she would rather be living the life of a warrior, doing great deeds and not worrying about courtship or men. However, the next day Sigurd visited Brynhild in her room, and she granted him entry to sit with her, an honor that few men besides her father had enjoyed.

Brynhild warned Sigurd that despite their love, it was not their fate to live together, for she was a shield-maiden and he was destined to marry another woman named Gudrun. But Sigurd assured Brynhild that no woman besides her could possibly tempt him, for she was the wisest and most beautiful woman in the world, and he kissed and embraced her. Despite her fears of the future she foresaw, Brynhild agreed that there was no man so brave and honorable as Sigurd and they did indeed belong together. They exchanged rings and swore oaths to each other, then Sigurd was again on his way, but he intended to return to his beloved Brynhild.

Shortly after Sigurd's departure, another guest sought out Brynhild's wisdom and foresight. This guest, who had traveled from a neighboring kingdom, was a great and beautiful woman, dressed all in gold, and she was the daughter of King Gjuki. This woman was plagued by disturbing dreams about marriage and loss, and she wished to consult the Valkyrie for advice and clarity. And of course, this beautiful woman was named Gudrun, and like Sigurd's uncle Gripir, Brynhild gave Gudrun her whole life story (full of spoilers; we'll get to it soon!)—and also like Sigurd, her fate was sealed, and she either didn't change it or didn't remember the details of her future.

GUNNAR

ALSO KNOWN AS: **GUNTHAR**
OLD NORSE TRANSLATION: **"WARRIOR"**
KEY FAMILY MEMBERS: SISTER **GUDRUN**; WIFE **BRYNHILD**

Gunnar is the next character who enters into this story within *The Saga of the Volsungs*. King Gjuki and his wife, the witch Grimhild, had three sons (Gudrun's brothers): Gunnar, Hogni, and Guttorm. The brothers were remarkable, but they were young and not as accomplished as Sigurd. Guttorm was not yet grown to adulthood, but Gunnar and Hogni had potential to be great men and only needed their courage to be tested to win renown.

THE STORY YOU NEED TO KNOW:

When Sigurd went riding into Gjuki's kingdom, his fame preceded him. The king and his sons were duly impressed and welcomed Sigurd. He shared meals with them in their hall, where he caught the eyes and ears of Grimhild. She heard him professing his love for Brynhild but knew his wealth and honor would be a great asset. So, she presented Sigurd with a horn filled with a magic drink that made him forget Brynhild and told Sigurd that she would like him to become a member of their family. Shortly thereafter, Gunnar convinced Sigurd to marry his beautiful sister

Gudrun, and Gunnar and Sigurd swore an oath of blood brother-hood to each other. Sigurd's wedding gift to Gudrun was a piece of Fafnir's heart to eat. But instead of learning the language of birds, it made Gudrun wiser...but also more malicious.

Sigurd, Gunnar, and Hogni banded together and went on some Viking raids, accomplishing great deeds. But when they returned home, Grimhild told Gunnar that it was time to settle down and find a wife. She told him to go after Brynhild and take Sigurd with him to help. They first went to Brynhild's father, King Buthli, and then her foster father, Heimir, and they got the same answer: They would support the marriage if only the proud Bryn-hild agreed to it, for she had sworn an oath to marry only a man with no fear, and to ensure this, she had surrounded her hall with a ring of fire. Only the bravest of men could get near her by riding through it.

Gunnar and Sigurd found Brynhild's ring of fire, and Gunnar tried to ride through it to reach her, but his horse refused to pass the fire. Gunnar asked Sigurd if he could borrow his horse Grani, the best of all horses, but Grani also refused with Gunnar on his back. Therefore, Sigurd decided that he would change appear-ances with Gunnar, and Sigurd-disguised-as-Gunnar on Grani had no trouble at all leaping through the ring of fire, and therein found Brynhild. He introduced himself as Gunnar and asked for her to consent to their marriage since he had now proven himself. Brynhild hesitated at first because she was still in love with Sig-urd and awaiting his return. But since she had made the vow, she realized that now she must honor it and consented to marry Gun-nar. Leaving Aslaug, the daughter she had secretly conceived with Sigurd, in the care of her foster father, Heimir, Brynhild went to marry Gunnar. Her father King Buthli and her brother Atli came to celebrate her wedding.

So now Sigurd and Gudrun, and Gunnar and Brynhild, were all under one roof in Gjuki's kingdom, celebrating their recent marriages. What could possibly go wrong? Well, for starters, when Sigurd saw Brynhild marry Gunnar, he suddenly remembered her and the oaths he had made to her. Brynhild and Gudrun started out friendly, but slowly Brynhild grew resentful of Gudrun's marriage to her true love Sigurd. Gudrun asked why Brynhild was so angry with her, and she told Gudrun how Grimhild had tricked Sigurd into forgetting her and how Sigurd had then tricked her into marrying Gunnar, despite his fear and weakness. The jealousy and rivalry between the two women grew until they were both desperately unhappy despite their wealthy kingdoms and accomplished husbands. Eventually, Brynhild claimed to be sick and went to her bed and refused to get up, eat, or drink. Gunnar visited his wife and tried to determine what was wrong.

Brynhild then told him everything. She knew all the tricks and lies, all the betrayals and failures. Gunnar warned her not to slander him, his sister Gudrun, or his mother, Grimhild, but Brynhild in her anger tried to kill him. His brother Hogni saw this and restrained her, but Gunnar didn't wish to see his wife in chains and set her free. She told him he'd never see her happy again, since she broke her own vow and married a lesser man, and she destroyed her prized golden tapestries, wailing so loudly that her cries could be heard throughout the whole town. Fearing for their safety, Gudrun asked Sigurd to try and bribe Brynhild against revenge with gold.

Sigurd went to Brynhild and tried to calm her wrath and pain by telling her that Gunnar was a great man and she could be happy with him if only she would let herself. But the conversation quickly dissolved, and they confessed their undying love and realized how miserable life was without each other. And yet, they could not break their vows of marriage and brotherhood to Gunnar without great dishonor. Sigurd's chest swelled with such agony that his chain mail burst, and he left but told Gunnar that Brynhild might speak to him. When Gunnar went to her, though, all she told him was that she hated him and couldn't bear to live anymore, and she warned him that he was on the verge of losing everything.

Desperate to avoid dishonor by divorce, but unable to break his blood-brother oath to Sigurd, Gunnar devised another plan: He went to his youngest brother, Guttorm, who was too young to swear a loyalty oath to Sigurd. Gunnar and Hogni told Guttorm of Sigurd's heinous crime (taking Brynhild's virginity) and asked him to kill Sigurd to spare the family the humiliating divorce. Grimhild gave Guttorm another enchanted drink to make him murderously aggressive, and after two failed attempts to gather the courage, he finally burst into Sigurd's bedroom while he and Gudrun slept and stabbed him through the heart. Sigurd woke and threw his sword Gram at Guttorm as he retreated, impaling him through the back.

Awaking at the clamor, covered in the blood of her husband and brother, Gudrun screamed so loud that the whole town could hear, including Brynhild, who could do nothing but laugh. At Sigurd's funeral, Brynhild threw herself on the pyre to burn alongside him (and his three-year-old son with Gudrun, who Brynhild had killed!) and followed him to Hel.

GUDRUN

ALSO KNOWN AS: GUÐRÚN, GUTHRUN

OLD NORSE TRANSLATION: "BATTLE," "SECRET"

KEY FAMILY MEMBERS: BROTHER GUNNAR; HUSBAND SIGURD;

LATER HUSBAND ATLI

It once seemed like Gudrun had everything going for her. She was beautiful and intelligent, born to a wealthy king, had honorable brothers capable of increasing their kingdom's strength, and was betrothed and married to the most famous warrior king who had ever lived. However, thanks to her wicked mother, jealous sister-in-law, and vengeful brother, poor Gudrun became Sigurd's widow. She felt unescapable sorrow after Sigurd was murdered by Gunnar and their young son was murdered by Brynhild. But Gudrun's story does not end there, and her continuing fate is described in *Guthrunarkvitha I, II,* and *III, Atlakvitha,* and *Guthrunarhvot* in the Poetic Edda as well as *The Saga of the Volsungs.*

THE STORY YOU NEED TO KNOW:

Following the death of Sigurd and her son, Gudrun wandered the woods in sorrow, wishing for death. By chance, she came to the hall of King Half, befriended his daughter Thora, and stayed with them for three years, weaving tapestries that depicted the great deeds of the Volsung family. But when Grimhild learned where her daughter was hiding, she asked Gunnar to go and compensate her for the loss of her husband and son. Gunnar agreed, and Grimhild went with him to ensure he succeeded.

Gudrun received her family but did not trust them. Grimhild made her another enchanted drink that made her forget Gunnar's crimes, and she agreed to return home with them. But even magic beer was not enough to make her forget losing Sigurd. Grimhild then tried to convince Gudrun to marry King Atli (Brynhild's brother), but she refused on the grounds that he was nowhere near as good a man as Sigurd. Grimhild angrily demanded that she remarry and Gudrun reluctantly agreed, though she knew no joy would come of this marriage and feared more great sadness awaited her.

The wedding feast was splendid, but Gudrun did not love her new husband. Atli began having nightmares and asked Gudrun to interpret them, but all she saw in his dreams were indications of arrogance and omens of doom. As time passed, Atli began to wonder about Sigurd's great treasure (which Gunnar and Hogni had divided between themselves). He invited Gunnar and Hogni to join him for a party, promising them gifts and a great feast. Gudrun suspected that Atli was up to something, so she carved a warning in runes for her brothers. The messenger Vigni noticed her secret message, and before delivering the message, he modified it to an eager invitation instead. Both brothers hesitated to accept the invitation, but their wives, Glaumvor and Kostbera, accidentally served them too much to drink that night, and Vigni managed to convince them, saying that Atli was old and wanted to leave his kingdom to his wife's younger brothers, who would better defend it. Kostbera later went to her husband, Hogni, and warned him that she had dreamed of great tragedy and suspected that the message from Gudrun was altered, but Hogni assured her that Atli was faithful.

The brothers arrived at King Atli's home and were greeted by an army. Realizing the deception, they beat Vigni to death and prepared to face Atli's army. When they came to Atli's courtyard, he offered them welcome if only they handed over Sigurd's treasure, which should now belong to Gudrun('s husband). They refused and prepared for battle. Gudrun heard the fighting and rushed to greet her brothers, realizing that her warning had failed. Gunnar and Hogni fought bravely but were outnumbered, captured, and imprisoned.

Atli's men interrogated Gunnar for the location of the hidden treasure, but he said he would tell them nothing until he saw his brother's heart. First, they cut the heart out of an enslaved person and showed it to Gunnar, but he knew it was not Hogni's heart when he saw how it trembled. They went back and tortured Hogni, but he was fierce and fearless, laughing as they cut his heart from his chest. They showed it to Gunnar, who saw that this was not a coward's heart, and knew it was his brother's. Gunnar then told Atli that he was now the only one who knew, and he would never tell. Enraged, Atli had Gunnar thrown in a snake pit, and he too showed courage facing death, as the largest viper dug its fangs into his heart.

Atli then went to Gudrun and mocked her, saying that she was the cause of her brothers' deaths. She bitterly told him that there was no way to repay her for killing her brothers, but now she had no other man to obey except him, and she allowed him to think that he had overpowered her. She requested that he prepare another feast to honor all their fallen kinsmen, and Atli agreed. Meanwhile, she plotted her revenge. She killed their two young sons, turned their skulls into goblets, mixed their blood with the wine, cooked their hearts on a spit, and served this to Atli at his feast. He ate and drank, and then she told him of her repayment for his cruelty. Atli was (rightly) horrified, and he threatened to stone her to death for her evil deeds.

Soon after, Gudrun conspired with Hogni's surviving son Niflung to avenge his father's death. Gudrun waited until Atli was drunk and asleep, then she stabbed him through the chest with a sword. Atli was startled awake by the strike and saw his wife standing over him, and he asked what he ever did to deserve this. Her family had blessed their marriage and he had paid the bride price, but she told him that he was a liar and a coward, and she could not endure being married to him after the best king who ever lived. According to *Atlakvitha*, she then sealed all the doors to Atli's halls, with herself, all his finest men, and their families inside, and burned it to the ground, and that was the end of the children of Gjuki.

But *The Saga of the Volsungs* tells us that Gudrun survived to suffer yet another tragedy: She threw herself in the river, which washed her ashore in King Jonakr's kingdom. He married her, and they had three sons whom they raised alongside Gudrun's beautiful young daughter with Sigurd, named Svanhild. An old man named King Jormunrekk sent his son Randver to propose to Svanhild on his behalf. But Randver and Svanhild fell in love on the voyage home, and when a messenger told the king that his son had slept with his new bride, he hanged his son and ordered

Svanhild to be trampled to death by horses. Gudrun then asked her three sons with Jonakr (Hamdir, Sorli, and Erp) to avenge their sister, but they were betrayed by Odin on the battlefield and stoned to death by Jormunrekk shortly after Gudrun herself lay down and finally died.

RAGNAR LOTHBROK

ALSO KNOWN AS: RAGNARR LODBROK, LOÐBRÓK

OLD NORSE TRANSLATION: RAGNAR: "COUNSEL,"
"ARMY"; LOTHBROK: "SHAGGY-PANTS"

KEY FAMILY MEMBERS: WIFE THORA; LATER WIFE ASLAUG;
SEVERAL SONS KNOWN COLLECTIVELY AS THE RAGNARSSONS

Ragnar Lothbrok is rivaled by few (arguably only Sigurd the Dragon Slayer) for the title of most renowned and famous hero in the Norse legends. Tales of his adventures are told in *The Saga of Ragnar Lothbrok*, Saxo Grammaticus's *The History of the Danes*, and several other texts. He is connected to the Volsung family via his marriage to his second wife, Aslaug (she gets her own story next!), but his heroic deeds began with his marriage to his first wife, Thora, and continued through his participation in adventures alongside his sons.

Saxo mentions an earlier wife named Ladgerda (also recorded as Lagertha, Lathgertha, or Ladgertha), but she is not included in any of the Old Norse documents, so we don't really know a whole lot about her. But what Saxo does briefly tell us is a rather compelling story (and perhaps why she became a main character in the *Vikings* television show that retells a much-embellished story of Ragnar's life, despite the fact that she's mentioned only briefly in the mythological sources): She was a fierce warrior in her own right and braver than most men. She caught Ragnar's attention in battle when her long hair hanging loose down her back revealed she was a woman. But trust is very important in any marriage, and he apparently ended up divorcing her when that trust eroded, especially after she sent him a pack of vicious beasts, hoping they would kill and eat him.

THE STORY YOU NEED TO KNOW:

Sigurd Ring was a great king of Denmark, famous for defeating and killing another king named Harald Wartooth. He had a wise and handsome son named Ragnar. As soon as he was old enough, Ragnar commanded a great army and fleet of ships, becoming an unequaled warrior. He was in Gotland one summer when a wealthy and powerful earl named Herruth had gotten himself into a bit of a bind. Herruth had a beloved daughter named Thora, who was more skilled and beautiful than any other woman, and he built her a house and frequently sent her gifts. One of these gifts was a small snake, which she let sit in a chest filled with gold. Unbeknownst to Thora and her father, this snake was in fact a baby dragon, and it grew in size (along with the pile of gold it was guarding) until it encircled her entire house and trapped her inside. No one would approach it except the man who had to feed it, and it ate an entire steer at every meal. The earl promised that any man who could kill this dragon would have earned the right to marry his daughter and could claim the growing pile of gold as a wedding gift.

Ragnar pretended he didn't hear the earl's announcement, but in secret he devised a special garment: He made himself some dark, shaggy pants, and he boiled them in a sticky pitch or resin, and then rolled around in the sand. While maybe not the most fashionable pants of the century, they would protect him from the dragon's poisonous blood and venom. He left his ship under cover of darkness armed with an unusually large spear, though he loosened the nail that held the point to the shaft. As he approached Thora's cabin, he saw the sleeping dragon and stabbed it through the back and then again through the heart. The point of his spear came loose on his second thrust and remained embedded in the dragon's heart. The blood splattered onto Ragnar, but his shaggy pants protected his skin from the poison. The dragon gave such a hideous cry that Thora's whole house shook, and she awoke and rushed out to see what had happened. She saw Ragnar vanishing into the darkness and called after him, asking his name and why he was leaving. He told her neither, instead giving her a poem with very little useful information, and so she went back to bed.

The next morning, the earl found the dragon dead with the spear point still in its heart. Thora told her father about the man she had seen in the shadows but could not identify. The earl decided to call a town meeting, and any man who did not attend would face his rage. He planned to inspect their spear shafts to see which would match the point still lodged in the dead dragon. Ragnar and all his men attended, not wishing to anger the earl, and it was soon discovered that Ragnar's spear shaft matched the point perfectly. Ragnar admitted to killing the dragon, and though he was only fifteen years old, he was married to Thora and won the gold as a reward.

There was a great wedding feast in their honor, and he took his bride home and ruled his kingdom. They loved each other, were happy, and produced two sons named Eirek and Agnar, who excelled as warriors like their father. But suddenly, Thora became ill and died, and Ragnar was so devastated by this loss that he no longer wished to rule his kingdom. He left his sons in charge and went away raiding, always victorious.

NOW YOU KNOW

"Lothbrok" is not a surname or last name, but rather an unusual nickname to commemorate the garment that allowed Ragnar to slay the dragon. His children are collectively referred to as the Ragnarssons, or the Sons of Ragnar (the "Shaggy-Pants" nickname doesn't transfer to his wives and children). In Viking-era Norse and Icelandic culture, a child inherited their last name from their parent's first name, so technically, Ragnar's last name would be Sigurdsson after his father, Sigurd Ring ("Ring" is also a nickname to distinguish him from other Sigurds). But "Shaggy-Pants" is a much more compelling and less confusing designation, given how common a name Sigurd was, and so that is how the great hero Ragnar is remembered by history.

ASLAUG

ALSO KNOWN AS: ASLÖG

OLD NORSE TRANSLATION: LOOSELY "GODLY," "BETROTHED"

KEY FAMILY MEMBERS: FATHER SIGURD; MOTHER BRYNHILD;
HUSBAND RAGNAR; SONS IVAR THE BONELESS AND SIGURD
SNAKE-EYE (TWO OF THE RAGNARSSONS)

Remember when Sigurd first found Brynhild sleeping in the ring of fire as punishment by Odin for killing the wrong king—and they fell in love with each other almost immediately? Well, according to *The Saga of the Volsungs*, Brynhild conceived a child of Sigurd's during this encounter, before her marriage to Gunnar. This daughter was named Aslaug, and she was left in the care of a foster father named Heimir following the separation and death of her parents. Aslaug's story actually starts *The Saga of Ragnar Lothbrok*, and her involvement with Ragnar continues after the death of Thora.

THE STORY YOU NEED TO KNOW:

When Aslaug was three years old, news reached Heimir that her parents had died. Heimir feared for Aslaug's safety, knowing the Volsung family had many jealous enemies who might try to wipe out the family line. He decided to hide her in a harp, along with some gold, and he wandered, disguised as a beggar musician. He fed her magic onions to keep her from being hungry, and soothed her with harp music when she cried. While traveling in Norway, he encountered a poor farmer's wife named Grima, who allowed him to spend the night but suggested that he sleep outside in the barn rather than in the house, since she knew she could be quite talkative.

And talkative she was: When her husband, Aki, came home, she told him about the traveler sleeping in the barn and tried to convince Aki to kill him and take whatever money he had. The farmer knew it was unwise to betray a guest who had been promised hospitality, but Grima nagged him until he finally agreed. Aki snuck into the barn with an ax, dealt one deadly blow to Heimir, and ran away. Heimir awakened and made such a scream that the whole barn collapsed and caused an earthquake. But Grima found the harp in the wreckage and broke it, finding inside the treasure and the girl, who refused to speak or tell them her name. Aki suspected this was bad fortune. Poor as they were, now they had another mouth to feed. But they agreed to raise her as their own. There was just one problem: This child was beautiful, and Grima and Aki were exceptionally ugly. No one would believe she was their child, so they named her Kraka ("crow") and covered her head in tar and dressed her in long hoods to conceal her beauty, a sign of noble origin.

Some years later, upon the death of Thora, Ragnar left his kingdom and went out raiding to distract himself from grief. While some of his men were ashore looking for supplies, they came to Grima's cabin and asked if she would help them bake bread. Grima said she was too old to help, but they could go find her daughter. They then met the unexpectedly lovely daughter of this hideously ugly woman, for no amount of clothing could hide her radiance. She helped them bake the bread, but they were so distracted that they burned it, and Ragnar was upset when his breakfast was terrible. He demanded to know what was wrong with his men, and they confessed that they'd encountered the most beautiful woman. Ragnar doubted she could be prettier than Thora, but he agreed to send some of his men to bring this girl to his boat and give her a riddle to see if she was also clever: Come neither clothed nor naked, fed nor starving, and not alone but with no other person.

The next day, Kraka came to him wrapped in fishing nets, using her own hair to hide her body, and chewing on an onion so that she was not fed but also not fully starved. Her dog accompanied her, so she was not alone. Ragnar was impressed by her cleverness and taken in by her beauty, but her dog bit his hand so his men jumped in and killed her dog. He tried to sleep with her, but she refused, saying she had only come to visit him upon his command. He offered her a marriage proposal, but Kraka told Ragnar that she was going home, though if he completed his planned journey and still desired to marry her, he should return and she would go with him then.

So that is exactly what he did. He returned and sent for Kraka. At sunrise, Kraka went to Grima and Aki and told them that she knew they had killed her foster father and though she would not hurt them, she cursed them that each day for the rest of their lives would be worse than the last. She then went to meet Ragnar on his ship. He immediately tried to sleep with her again, but she refused until they were married. So he rushed back to the kingdom, they got married, and he tried to sleep with her again on their wedding night. She told him he should wait a few days, saying that if they consecrated their marriage too quickly, their first child would be born without bones. But he didn't hold back his desire and ignored her warning, and sure enough, their first child was Ivar the Boneless.

Ragnar's further adventures brought him to the hall of a friendly Swedish king named Eystein, who offered Ragnar his daughter named Ingibjorg. His men suggested he divorce his peasant wife Kraka and marry the powerful king's daughter, and eventually, he agreed this was wise. Kraka knew something was wrong when he came home, and she decided she would finally reveal her true identity to her husband: She identified herself as Aslaug, daughter of the great hero Sigurd and the Valkyrie Brynhild, a far greater lineage than Ingibjorg's. To prove it, she said that their next son would have "snake-eyes," and sure enough, the son she was carrying was born with a snake eye. They named him Sigurd Snake-Eye, Ragnar called off his marriage to Ingibjorg, and he continued to live happily with Aslaug.

THE SONS OF RAGNAR

ALSO KNOWN AS: **THE RAGNARSSONS**

Ragnar Lothbrok's children were an army in their own right. His first sons (with Thora) were Agnar and Eirek. We have also met Ivar (the Boneless) and Sigurd (Snake-Eye), his oldest and youngest sons with Aslaug, and they had a few more sons in the middle: Rognvald, Bjorn (Ironside), and Hvitserk. Each of them grew to be a great Viking warrior like their father, but it's through Sigurd Snake-Eye that the Volsung story continues.

THE STORY YOU NEED TO KNOW:

When Ragnar broke off his engagement to King Eystein's daughter, their friendship ended with Eystein feeling betrayed and dishonored. When Agnar and Eirek heard this, they decided that since the alliance had already dissolved, they might as well assemble an army and raid the Swedes. They landed in Sweden and began wreaking havoc, but Eystein assembled his own army—including the fearsome cow Sibilja, to whom the Swedes made many sacrifices. Eystein challenged the Ragnarssons' army with Sibilja leading the charge, and this cow let loose such a dreadful and horrible moo that the advancing soldiers lost their senses in terror and began fighting each other instead of their enemies.

Only Agnar and Eirek were able to withstand the accursed mooing, fighting with such fearless prowess that they cut through the ranks of Eystein's army several times. Eventually, Agnar fell, and his brother redoubled his efforts, not caring if he died. But Eirek was then captured, and Eystein offered him a truce, which included marrying his daughter off to Ragnar's son instead. But Eirek refused any payment and insisted on dying honorably. Though he accepted the truce on behalf of his men so they would be allowed to return to Ragnar's kingdom, he asked Eystein to set up a bed of spears that he might then throw himself upon and join his brother. Eystein agreed, and before Eirek died, he gave his men a ring to bring back to his stepmother, Aslaug.

When Eirek's men returned to Aslaug and informed her of Agnar's and Eirek's deaths, for the first time in her life, she wept a single blood-red tear. Ragnar and his other sons had also been out raiding, but when Ivar and his brothers returned, they went to their mother and exchanged news. Ivar told her how her son Rognvald had died, and she responded that he had gone to Odin and could not have died more honorably. But Aslaug then told Ivar of the deaths of Agnar and Eirek, and how she expected that he would avenge them. But Ivar hesitated, knowing full well the dark magic of Sibilja, and told his mother that it was not worth the risk. Aslaug was disappointed, but then three-year-old Sigurd Snake-Eye told his mother that he would accompany her, and none could stand against them.

Not wanting to be shown up by their toddler brother, Ivar, Bjorn, and Hvitserk changed their minds and readied a fleet. Aslaug insisted on accompanying them to judge how hard they tried to avenge their half-brothers. Not wanting their mom on their ships with them, they asked Aslaug to lead foot soldiers over land while they attacked from the sea, and she agreed. Changing her name to Randalin, a name evoking shields and befitting a Valkyrie's daughter, she met her sons in battle against Eystein and his dreadful cow. Ivar told his men to throw him at the cow, and he landed upon it with such force that he shattered all of the cow's bones. The Ragnarssons regrouped and succeeded in killing King Eystein, and Randalin returned home. Her sons decided to do more raiding, taking young Sigurd Snake-Eye with them wherever they went.

While his sons were away, Ragnar became bored and decided he'd overtake all of England with just two ships. Randalin informed him this was a very bad idea, but he wouldn't be dissuaded. As they parted, she gave him a shirt woven from a single long grey hair, and when he wore it, nothing could pierce him. Armed with the spear he used to kill Thora's dragon and shielded by his protective shirt from Randalin, Ragnar ravaged England, winning victory wherever he went. But when King Ella of Northumbria heard of the invasion, he assembled a massive army to fight Ragnar. All of Ragnar's men were killed, yet still Ragnar fought unscathed until finally he was captured. When Ella asked his name, Ragnar refused to answer, so they tortured him in a snake pit, but the snakes refused to bite until they removed his special shirt. As the vipers attacked, Ragnar bravely spoke his famous last words: "How the piglets would squeal if they saw the old boar now!" (Jackson Crawford's translation, *The Saga of the Volsungs,* copyright © 2017). And sure enough, when Ivar, Bjorn, Hvitserk, and Sigurd heard their father had been killed, they plotted a brutal revenge.

Ivar went to Ella and asked for payment: as much land as he could stretch a hide over. Ella agreed and Ivar cut a hide into thin strips, stretching it over miles of land, and there he built a mighty fortified kingdom called London. He gained the support of King Ella's people with unparalleled generosity and sent word to his brothers to bring the biggest army Denmark could muster. They overthrew and captured King Ella, and then sentenced him to death by way of the Blood Eagle (see sidebar). Ivar kept England, and the other brothers returned to Scandinavia and divided up their father's kingdom.

Now You Know

What is the Blood Eagle, exactly? It is a gruesome method of torture: The victim would be laid down prone on their stomach, and one by one, their ribs would be cut out and ripped from their spine to create the most exquisitely painful set of eagle wings protruding from the person's back. There's no archaeological evidence of this ritual being practiced in real life (or if it was, it might have been a more mundane version, like leaving bodies facedown on the battlefield for carrion birds to eat).

KING HARALD

Here we come to the end of the legendary *Saga of the Volsungs* and *The Saga of Ragnar Lothbrok.* Sigurd Snake-Eye had a daughter named Ragnhild, who had a son named Harald Fairhair. To recap his family tree back a bit further, Sigurd Snake-Eye was the son of Ragnar and Aslaug, who was the daughter of Sigurd the Dragon Slayer, who was the son of Sigmund, son of Volsung, son of Rerir, son of Sigi, who was a mortal son of Odin himself. So why is this noteworthy? Because Harald Fairhair was probably a real guy. A historical king of the Viking era, he is credited with the unification of Norway in the year 872. Granted, historical records of him pose some of the same issues as the Eddas and sagas: They were written generations later, and there are details of his life that don't line up among various versions, but twelfth- and thirteenth-century Nordic historians and poets were quite sure that he was real and that he succeeded in uniting the kingdom of Norway, though it fractured again following his death sometime around 930.

Because these later Icelandic writers were living in a society that had already exchanged its belief in gods like Odin for a mainstream devotion to Christianity, there's something to be said for their continued reverence of a mighty king who was claimed to be a descendant of a pagan god. For some writers, this could be interpreted as a divine right to rule and could elevate their political status (what we might today call Norwegian nationalism or Icelandic exceptionalism) with tales of heroic Viking ancestors. For others, like Snorri Sturluson, this was an inconvenient discrepancy with the Christian faith. Snorri tries to explain away this problem of interactions between humans and pagan gods in his prologue to the Prose Edda, one of the rare cases where Snorri departs from his source manuscripts and deliberately fabricates: He decides that Odin, Thor, and the other Aesir are in fact Trojans from Turkey who traveled to Sweden (where their names were changed for easier pronunciation in Old Norse) and were so magnificent that they were worshiped as gods by his Norse ancestors. These debates surrounding the true nature of Harald Fairhair continue into the twenty-first century.

THE STORY YOU NEED TO KNOW:

In his history of the Norse kings, *Heimskringla*, Snorri tells the story of how Harald unified Norway. After the death of his father, Halvdan the Black, Harald became a king at the age of ten. He and his uncle, Duke Guthorm, were fearsome Vikings who terrorized the region of Upland, conquering other Swedish kings and growing their kingdom. When Harald wished to marry, he sent messengers to a woman named Gyda, the daughter of King Eric of Hordaland. Though she had a reputation for being attractive, she was also quite spirited. She scoffed at the messengers and said she would not waste herself on a king who had such a small kingdom as Harald. She'd do better with someone like King Gorm in Denmark, or King Eric of Uppsala, for their kingdoms were far more impressive.

The messengers brought her response back to Harald, thinking that he would be angry and punish her for this insult. But instead, he took her words to heart, and emboldened by her challenge, he vowed that he would not stop—and neither would he brush nor cut his hair—until all of Norway paid him tribute. His strategy was a scorched-earth policy: Everywhere he went, his armies killed all the men who stood against them and burned their homes. Word spread, and while some fled into the woods to hide at his approach, others sought him out to preemptively surrender, willing to submit to his rule and pay his taxes instead of losing their lives and homes. He fought battle after battle with the kings who opposed him, and he gained victory after victory with his growing army. In his wake, he appointed trusted earls who were loyal to him to maintain his hold over conquered lands.

But Harald did not stop with Norway and sent his men to secure loyalty to his crown from the Vikings and settlers who populated the nearby islands: the Faroes, Shetlands, Orkneys, and Hebrides. He finally remembered that strong-willed woman who had told him his kingdom was not large enough, and since he was king of all Norway, he sent his messengers to Gyda again. This time his marriage proposal was accepted. They married and had five sons together (though by the end of his rule, it's said that he had married and divorced nine women), and he continued battling to maintain his hold over this massive kingdom. All this time, he'd been called Harald Thick-Hair or Tangle-Hair, but ten years later, when he finally truly felt like he had subdued all of Norway and fulfilled his oath, he took a bath and had his hair combed. It was then so beautiful that his best friend, an earl named Ragnvald, gave him the befitting new name, Harald Fairhair.

HROLF KRAKI

ALSO KNOWN AS: HROÐULF KRAGE
OLD NORSE TRANSLATION: HROLF: "WOLF";
KRAKI: "THIN," "POLE"

Hrolf was a legendary Danish king who appears throughout several texts: In addition to his own legendary saga, *The Saga of Hrolf Kraki and His Champions*, he is mentioned in the Prose and Poetic Eddas in kennings, and his story is retold in pieces and variants in Saxo's *The History of the Danes* as well as the epic poem *Beowulf*. He was a berserker, a semi-supernatural soldier of exceptional skill widely feared in the Norse texts. His saga is more episodic than others, with many characters loosely related or unrelated to Hrolf himself, but much of his story revolves around conflicts that began with his parents.

THE STORY YOU NEED TO KNOW:

There was once a proud queen named Olof, who insisted on living like a king. She was violent and greedy and did not wish to marry. But a king named Helgi (not the same Helgi of the Volsung line!) decided that he wanted to marry her to increase his own wealth and honor, and he marched on her kingdom with an army in secret. He showed up at her door before she could assemble a defensive army and demanded either a battle or a wedding feast. Out of options, Queen Olof agreed to the wedding feast; but when King Helgi got so drunk he passed out, she shaved his hair, covered him with tar, shoved him in an ugly animal hide bag that she had sewn, and sent him back to his ships. Dishonored, he got revenge by convincing her enslaved person to bring her out to the woods in the middle of the night with the promise of treasure, where he captured her, brought her back to his ship, and raped her repeatedly over several days before he let her go.

She became pregnant and gave birth to a beautiful girl named Yrsa, who she sent to live with a poor farmer. Yrsa had no knowledge of her noble parentage, and one day, King Helgi met her, disguised as a beggar. Consumed by desire for her, he took her away (also against her will) and married her, not realizing she was his daughter. Queen Olof let this happen, knowing it would bring Helgi further shame. Helgi and Yrsa had a son together named Hrolf, and when the time was ripe, Queen Olof told Helgi and Yrsa that they were father and daughter. Appalled by this, Yrsa left Helgi in misery, and Olof married her daughter off to another king named Adils to infuriate Helgi further.

Helgi traveled to Uppsala to meet King Adils and attempt to win Yrsa back. They greeted him and invited him to a feast, but Adils secretly had an army ready to ambush Helgi when he returned to his ships that night. Helgi was slain, and Yrsa was distraught, for she had grown to love him before she was aware of their incest. Meanwhile, Hrolf had become a great king in his father's absence and decided that he would avenge his father's death by meeting with King Adils and demanding compensation. He assembled a team of twelve champion soldiers, twelve berserkers, and an army, and readied their expedition to Uppsala. Along the way, they encountered a mysterious farmer, who somehow magically managed to provide lodging and food for the whole army (yes, it's Odin in disguise!). This farmer offered Hrolf advice: Send the army home and meet Adils in combat with just the berserkers.

Hrolf took his advice, and when they arrived at Adils's hall, they were welcomed. But Adils was treacherous and started to test Hrolf and his champions over dinner. Men jumped out at them from behind tapestries, but Hrolf and his champions slayed them all. He then set their seats on fire, but they did not flee from the flames and instead threw several of Adils's troops into the fire to stoke it. They tried to throw Adils himself in, too, but he escaped and ran into Yrsa, who shamed him for betraying both her ex-husband and son. Yrsa went to her son Hrolf and greeted him and his champions warmly, and her servant Vogg gave him the name "Kraki" because his face was thin as a pole.

That night, Adils tried another plan. He made sacrifices to an enormous boar, set this formidable beast on Hrolf and his champions, and lit their house on fire. But Hrolf's dog defeated the boar, and Hrolf and his soldiers ran out of the burning house with their weapons at the ready. They were again victorious against Adils's army, but he hid, escaping like a coward.

Yrsa gave her son the treasure he was rightfully owed for the death of his father, and as they were leaving, King Adils saw them taking off with his gold. He followed them angrily, and when he bent down to pick up a ring that Hrolf had dropped, Hrolf cut off his buttocks and forced him to retreat in shame, weak with blood loss and humiliated by the injury. Hrolf went home and lived as a great king in dignity and honor until he was eventually betrayed by his sister Skuld, who convinced her husband to overtake her brother's kingdom with the help of her witchcraft. But his berserkers eventually captured and tortured her, and Hrolf's kingdom was rightfully restored to his daughters.

Now You Know

Old Norse and contemporary English are closely related languages. It's not surprising that the Old Norse "berserker" is the root of the English word "berserk"—but just like "bear" and "bare" are homophones in modern English, they're equally close in Old Norse, so researchers are not certain which word is referenced in the terminology for these super-soldiers. Were they men who fought with the ferocious tenacity of bears or perhaps wore bear skins into battle? Or were they men so skilled and fearless that they fought bare, without armor or perhaps even shirts, in their bare skin? Either way, sources agree that berserkers were the most fearsome of warriors.

HERVOR

ALSO KNOWN AS: **HERVÖR, HERVǪR; PSEUDONYM: HERVARD**
OLD NORSE TRANSLATION: **HERVARD: "ARMY," "GUARD"**
KEY FAMILY MEMBERS: **FATHER ANGANTYR; HUSBAND HOFUND;**
SONS HEIDREK AND ANGANTYR

Hervor is one of the rare female Vikings in the literature, and her story, *The Saga of Hervor and Heidrek*, begins with her forefathers and their acquisition of the magic sword Tyrfing. Her behavior as a young woman often led to her being scolded and condemned by the other characters, though ironically these behaviors reflect the ideals for which young men in her day would have been praised. Oscillating between the gender roles assigned to men and women, Hervor reminds us that no matter who you are and what you do, no one can escape a curse once it is put into effect.

THE STORY YOU NEED TO KNOW:

Hervor's father was named Angantyr, and he and his twelve brothers were berserkers. When one of his brothers, Hjorvard, swore an oath to marry a Swedish king's daughter, the brothers traveled to Sweden to make good on this oath. But the daughter in question was courted by another man as well, named Hjalmar, and the king let his daughter choose between Hjorvard the

berserker (who she knew nothing about) and Hjalmar the soldier (who had long been loyal to her father).

Much to Hjorvard's disappointment, she chose Hjalmar, so he challenged him to a duel. As the brothers left to duel, their father handed Angantyr his sword, Tyrfing. Once drawn, Tyrfing could not be resheathed until it had drawn blood, and no one could survive an injury, no matter how small a cut. The ensuing duel was epic, and the thirteen berserkers, Hjalmar, and his men all "showed each other the way to Valhalla" (Jackson Crawford's translation, *Two Sagas of Mythical Heroes*, copyright © 2021). Angantyr and his brothers were laid in burial mounds on the island of Samso, and Tyrfing was buried with him.

Some time later, Angantyr's wife, Svava, gave birth to a girl, and they named her Hervor. She grew up in the house of her grandfather, the earl Bjarmar, and her mother never told her who her father was. But although Hervor was especially beautiful, she was also especially wicked: Instead of weaving tapestries, she practiced archery and challenged men in the woods to duels (in which she always succeeded in killing the men and winning their money). The earl finally sent an army after Hervor to bring her back home and make her behave, but she was provoked by an enslaved person who told her that she was no better than them, for her father was a pig herder who slept with her mother, the earl's daughter.

Furious at this insult, Hervor went to her mother and grandfather and demanded to know if this was true. Bjarmar finally confessed that Hervor's father was Angantyr, a great berserker buried on the island of Samso. She asked her mother to make her fine clothing that she'd make for a son, and Hervor dressed as a man, called herself Hervard, and went out to reclaim her father's wealth and riches. She became the leader of a group of Vikings and told them that they were going to Samso to look for treasures in the graves of the berserkers.

But none of her men were brave enough to go with her, telling her that it was unwise to travel to such a place from which none ever returned alive. She called them cowards and went alone to the island, where she found many grave fires burning. Standing before Angantyr's grave, she called to him and woke him from the dead, cursing him to sit whole in his grave, never reaching Valhalla, unless he gave his only child her rightful inheritance: his magic sword Tyrfing.

Angantyr's burial mound opened and he arose from the flames to answer her, telling her to go back to her ships. He told her that Tyrfing was cursed and would destroy her whole family, causing tragic conflict between her sons. They argued for a while, until Hervor convinced her father not only of her courage but also her stubbornness: She was not leaving without Tyrfing.

He finally relented but reminded her that the sword was cursed and she was doomed. Hervor left the island with the sword and resumed her Viking identity as Hervard until she grew wealthy, successful, and bored. Eventually, she returned to the home of her mother and grandfather and took up weaving and sewing as a young woman should. This new well-behaved Hervor was courted by a king named Hofund, and they married and had two sons. She named her first son Angantyr after her father and the second Heidrek. For a while, they lived happily, and she ignored the cursed sword Tyrfing and the warnings she had received from her father's ghost. Angantyr grew up to be like his father, wise and good-tempered, and Hofund favored him. Heidrek, however, was reckless with a mean streak, the spitting image of his mother in her Viking days, and therefore Hervor loved Heidrek best.

HEIDREK

ALSO KNOWN AS: **HEIÐREK**
OLD NORSE TRANSLATION: **"HONOR," "RULER"**
KEY FAMILY MEMBERS: **MOTHER HERVOR; BROTHER ANGANTYR**

Heidrek was Hervor's favorite son. While his brother, Angan-tyr, inherited the wisdom of their father, Hofund, Heidrek took after his mother's side of the family: violent and rash. Because of his father's favoritism toward his brother, Heidrek acted out and invited the trouble that Hervor was cursed to bring upon her family when she acquired the magic sword Tyrfing.

THE STORY YOU NEED TO KNOW:

King Hofund held a feast one day and invited everyone except Heidrek. Heidrek decided to attend anyway and cause trouble, to get revenge on his dad for the insult. His brother, Angantyr, invited him to sit next to him, but every time Angantyr got up, Heidrek started fights between the men seated around them until one man drunkenly killed another. Hofund knew Heidrek was behind the mischief and kicked him out. As he walked home, Heidrek in his anger took a giant rock and threw it in the direction of the courtyard, where some men could be heard talking in the dark. When he went back to check if his rock had done any damage, he found that he had accidentally (well, it wasn't really an accident, was it?) killed his own brother. When he confessed to Hofund what he had done, he was disowned and banished, though Hervor tried, unsuccessfully, to change her husband's mind. But if he had to leave with no possessions, Hervor asked Hofund to at least give the boy some good advice to take with him, and so he did:

- Don't help anyone who has betrayed their own lord.
- Don't free a murderer.
- Don't let your wife visit her relatives too often.
- Don't stay out late sleeping around with concubines.
- If you're in a rush, don't ride your best horse.
- Don't take in foster children of higher class than you are.

Before he left, Hervor went to her son in secret and gave him her magic sword, Tyrfing, which she had wisely kept hidden. The rest of his saga describes Heidrek, armed and angry, going out of his way to disregard his father's advice out of spite. The first person he encountered on his journey was a man with a prisoner who had betrayed his own lord, and Heidrek paid for the criminal's freedom. He soon thereafter met another captive who had murdered a friend, and Heidrek freed him too.

Heidrek ended up in the service of a king named Harald, but there was great unrest in this kingdom. Heidrek offered to lead an army against those disloyal to King Harald, and none could stand against Heidrek and Tyrfing. As a reward for his victory, King Harald said he would give Heidrek anything he wanted. So, he asked for the hand of the king's daughter Helga, and they were married and had a son together—and he named his son Angantyr. But during a famine, it was prophesized that no harvest would come until the highest born son in the land was killed. Harald and Heidrek bickered about whose son should be sacrificed, and finally they sought out the advice of the wisest man they knew: Hofund.

Hofund decided that Heidrek's son was higher born, and so the child must be sacrificed—but he should demand in compensation every fourth man who was present at the sacrifice. The two men agreed to this, but now that Heidrek commanded a quarter of Harald's army, instead of sacrificing Angantyr, Heidrek waged war against Harald and killed him. Helga then hung herself in grief over the loss of her father. Heidrek went out pillaging with his army, breaking more of his father's advice, like sleeping around late at night with concubines. He settled down again with a Saxon king's daughter, married her, and let her travel home to visit her relatives as often as she wished. But when he returned unexpectedly from a raid, he caught her in bed with a handsome boy who was enslaved to her father, and he divorced her.

Heidrek agreed to foster the son of another king, and he instructed the boy to hide on a hunting trip. Heidrek came home upset, and when his concubine, Sifka, wanted to know why, he lied and told her that he had pulled out Tyrfing to cut an apple from a tree, but suddenly remembering the curse, Heidrek had realized that Tyrfing must now kill either himself or the boy before it could be put away, and so he killed his foster son to save himself. Sifka told the king that his son was dead, and Heidrek was sentenced to death—but the boy ran in just in time to prove the concubine was lying. Embarrassed, the king offered Heidrek a consolation prize, but Heidrek said he had no shortage of wealth or land, so the only thing he would accept was the king's daughter. As he rushed to move Sifka out to make room for his new wife, he rode his best horse. As he was carrying Sifka across the river, his best horse collapsed, and Sifka drowned.

Despite intentionally flouting all his father's advice, it was a riddle contest with Odin that was ultimately Heidrek's doom. Odin used his trademark unbeatable riddle: What did Odin whisper to Balder on his funeral pyre? Angry at his defeat, Heidrek pulled Tyrfing out and thrust it at Odin, who turned into a falcon and flew away, but Heidrek just managed to hit his tail feathers. Odin cursed Heidrek to be killed dishonorably and, sure enough, one night while he was sleeping, the men Heidrek had enslaved (whom he had probably treated quite poorly, knowing Heidrek!) broke into his bedroom, stole Tyrfing, and killed him with his own sword...because no one can escape a curse!

EGIL ONE-HAND

OLD NORSE TRANSLATION: "SWORD'S EDGE"

Egil was a great Viking hero who teamed up with another warrior named Asmund in *The Saga of Egil One-Hand and Asmund Berserkers-Slayer*. This saga features several stories within the main story, where these two young men must tell their family histories to entertain a Jotun woman in exchange for a meal and a bed on their journey.

THE STORY YOU NEED TO KNOW:

There was once a powerful king named Tryggve who had two very beautiful daughters, and they were both named Hild. One day while out walking, the eldest Hild (called Brynhild because she was a shield-maiden) was captured in the forest by a giant, ugly hare that carried her off. The king was bereaved and searched for her, hoping to find her in time for the magnificent feast he was planning. He called for his younger Hild (called Bekhild, a talented seamstress), but as she was walking through the garden to meet him, a large vulture came and carried her off too. Distraught, the king offered great rewards to anyone who could find his beloved daughters and bring them back, dead or alive.

The following summer, a young and wealthy Viking named Asmund came to stay with the king, and while there, word reached them of a menace terrorizing the kingdom named Egil One-Hand, and Asmund vowed to stop Egil as repayment for the king's hospitality. Asmund and Egil met in battle and were impressed by each other, and they decided that instead of risking all their men's lives, they would duel themselves. They fought to exhaustion, but they were too equally matched. The next day they woke up and fought again, and again, and again, until Asmund finally defeated Egil. But instead of killing him, he offered him blood brotherhood, and they returned together to King Tryggve. Egil vowed to help defend the kingdom, and after a year had passed, still with no word of the king's daughters, Egil and Asmund promised to find them. On their long journey, they met a Jotun mother and daughter who took them in for the night.

While they waited for the porridge to cook, the women asked Asmund and Egil about themselves. Asmund told them how he had achieved the title "Berserker's Bane": He had previously sworn blood brotherhood to a man named Aran, who became a king. Aran promised Asmund half of everything he owned, but when Aran was killed, Asmund sat with him in his burial mound for three days (until Aran resurrected, ran out of other food in his grave, and tried to eat Asmund—that ended his vigil abruptly!). Berserkers had overtaken Aran's kingdom while Asmund was away, and when he returned to reclaim his half, he did so—quite literally—over their dead bodies.

Egil then told his story. When he was twelve, he was winning a swimming race when a fog set in so thick that he could not see. He swam until he hit land, where he was captured by a Jotun who threatened to kill him if he did not tend the Jotun's goats for the rest of his life. Egil agreed, but after a year he ran away. The Jotun found him, dragged him back, chained massive rocks to his legs, and put him back to work for another seven years. Egil found a cat in the woods one day and brought it back to their cave. He bragged to the Jotun about the animal's magic golden eyes that could see in the dark and showed him the cat's eyes glowing in the firelight. The Jotun was intrigued, so Egil promised that if the Jotun removed the chains, he would lend him the golden eyes. Egil tied him down to perform the surgery, but instead he stabbed the Jotun's eyes out. The Jotun blocked his escape, trapping him in the cave, so Egil killed a goat and hid in its skin, waiting silently until the Jotun had to let the goats out. Hearing his human footsteps, the Jotun tried to catch him, but Egil just barely escaped. Defeated, he offered Egil a gold ring as a parting gift for his years of service; but when Egil reached out to take the ring, the Jotun cut his arm.

Despite his wound, he became a successful Viking captain. One day, he got involved in a fight between a Jotun man and a troll woman over a gold ring. Just as the Jotun was getting the upper hand, Egil cut his arm to help the woman, but the Jotun turned around and cut Egil's hand off at the wrist—taking his sword with it. Egil escaped in excruciating pain. He later met a young dwarf boy, who in exchange for gold forged him a special sword attached to his arm to replace his missing hand.

After telling stories, they finally ate and slept, and in the morning, they asked the Jotun women if they knew anything about the king's missing daughters. One of them said there was a powerful Jotun who had died, and his brothers fought over his kingdom.

So they had made a bet that whoever could capture the most famous king's daughter would win the kingdom, and the girls were made to compete in their crafts so the brothers could judge who had captured the better daughter, and when it was settled, they'd force the girls to marry them. Before the two men went on their way, the Jotun mother showed them one more thing: In her treasure hoard, she had Egil's hand in a box! With healing herbs, she reattached it, and helped them sneak into the Jotun kingdom to rescue the king's daughters. Disguised as servants, they broke up the Jotun's weddings, killed the kidnappers, and brought the daughters back to their father, who was overjoyed. Egil married Bekhild, and Asmund married Brynhild, with much celebration. Asmund returned home to his father's land and became king and lived a long and glorious life—until Odin himself slayed him in battle—while Egil inherited King Tryggve's kingdom upon his death.

FRODI

ALSO KNOWN AS: FRODI, FROTHI, FRODE, FRODO
OLD NORSE TRANSLATION: "LEARNED," "WISE"

Frodi was a legendary Danish king of the Skjoldungs family line, appearing in the Eddas, Snorri's *Ynglinga Saga* in *Heimskringla*, as well as Saxo's *The History of the Danes*. Like Hrolf Kraki, Frodi also shows up as a character in the Old English poem *Beowulf*. But what makes Frodi so unusual in the Norse literature is that he is one of the only kings not celebrated for his glorious conquests and victories in battle. Rather, he is known for ushering in a golden era of peace and plenty, so much so that Snorri associates him rather blatantly with Frey and fertility. While details of his lineage and the timeframe in which he reigned appear differently across sources, his accomplishment of "Frodi's Peace" is often agreed to coincide with the birth of Christ and the Pax Romana, another demonstration of how the manuscript writers rendered the pre-Christian texts in a manner that aligned with their own sensibilities.

THE STORY YOU NEED TO KNOW:

According to Saxo's *The History of the Danes*, the great king Frodi established his rule over much of Scandinavia and extended his kingdom out toward the Huns in the east and the British Isles in the west. The people were so contented that they would not steal golden rings from the king, even when he dropped them along the highway to test them. This period of his reign, known as Frodi's Peace, lasted for thirty years.

According to Snorri's *Ynglinga Saga*, during this time many sacrifices were made to Frey, and there were plentiful harvests. Frodi was helpful to other kings who needed aid in avenging wrongs, but in his kingdom, only an occasional accident upset the tranquility. He hosted magnificent feasts with extensive guest lists, but one guest in particular, named Fjolnir, partied a little too hard. He got so drunk off Frodi's mead that he could barely stay upright and lost all his senses. He was led to his bedroom that night, but got up to look for a bathroom while he was still drunk and sleepy. He tripped and fell from the loft and drowned to death in Frodi's giant mead vat.

Now Frodi's subjects may have appreciated thirty years of peace and prosperity, but who didn't have anything to gain from peace? Odin, who was counting on men to kill each other in battle so that he could scoop them up for his afterlife army of the dead, of course! In *Beowulf*, Frodi was slain after a long feud with his brother Halfdan (though in the Old Norse sources, Frodi was often called the father of Halfdan), but the version of Frodi's demise in *Skaldskaparmal* in the Prose Edda and the *Grottasongr* of the Poetic Edda is a bit more consistent with the other stories in Norse mythology. A mysterious traveler named Hangjaw came to Frodi, and he gave Frodi a magic millstone called the Grotti, which could grind out whatever was asked of it. But it was so heavy that no one could turn it. Another mysterious traveler named Spellcaster crossed Frodi's path in Sweden and sold him two women to serve as slaves, who were exceptionally large and strong and just might be able to turn that millstone.

These two women were named Fenja and Menja, and Frodi instructed them to grind out gold, peace, and joy. But he permitted them no rest from this toil, saying they could only stop grinding for the amount of time a cuckoo could be silent or the length of time it took to sing a song. What Frodi didn't know, however, was that both Hangjaw and Spellcaster were Odin in disguise, and he'd been set up to fail: Fenja and Menja were descendants of Jotun royalty, listing Hrungnir and Thiassi among their relatives, and they were not only angry about being treated so harshly but also powerful enough to do something about it.

One night, while Frodi was sleeping peacefully on fluffy pillows surrounded by gold, these two Jotun women stopped grinding out peace, happiness, and wealth. Instead, they ground out an army to betray Frodi. This army was joined by a Viking captain named Mysing, who killed Frodi and took all his possessions, including the Grotti and his two enslaved miller women. Mysing told them to grind out salt, and so they did—but they ground out so much salt that the ships sank, and a whirlpool formed in the sea that spun around and around like a millstone. And that was the end of Frodi and his golden era of peace.

Now You Know

It's quite fitting that Tolkien would borrow the anglicized spelling of Froði (Frodo) for a hobbit hero in The Lord of the Rings because of King Frodi's peaceful disposition. In addition to having a pacifist society, Tolkien's hobbits are particularly hungry fellows, too, so Frodo would most likely be pleased to know his namesake kept his subjects well-fed. Tolkien echoes Frodi's story in Frodo's interaction with Faramir (Boromir's nerdy brother with a gentler temperament), who refuses to take the cursed ring from Frodo, vowing never to touch it even if he found it lying by a highway—thus passing the Norse king Frodi's test.

SNORRI STURLUSON

ALSO KNOWN AS: SNORRE STURLESON, SNORRI STURLSON
OLD NORSE TRANSLATION: SNORRI: "ONSLAUGHT";
STURLUSON: "SON OF STURLA"
KEY FAMILY MEMBERS: FATHER STURLA; WIFE HERDIS;
LATER WIFE HALLVEIG

Snorri was a man who by this point probably needs little introduction. One of the most famous poets and writers of his time, Snorri wrote the Prose Edda, based on his study of earlier Norse poetry, as well as *Heimskringla*, the Lives of the Norse Kings. He compiled and recorded an extensive repertoire of Nordic history and mythology, and several other works have been potentially attributed to him, though authorship is difficult to verify. He was also quite a character with an interesting story in his own right, because every once in a while, truth can be just as fantastic as fiction.

THE STORY YOU NEED TO KNOW:

Snorri was born in Iceland in 1179 to Sturla Thordarson and Gudny Bodvarsdottir. When he was very young, his father, Sturla, was involved in a lawsuit with a man named Pall. At some point, Pall's wife became impatient and enraged and attacked Sturla with a knife, saying she was going to make him look like his one-eyed hero Odin, but the blow was deflected and hit the side of his face instead. Recognizing the insult, but not wanting to deal out harsher punishment that would have Pall and his wife living as beggars, a member of the Norwegian royal family named Jon Loftsson offered to compensate Sturla by raising and educating his son Snorri. Thus was the beginning of Snorri's relationship to the royal family of Norway.

In Jon's care, Snorri received an excellent education and became a renowned poet and lawyer. Eventually, his father died, his mother ran out of money after squandering his inheritance, and his foster father, Jon, died as well. The solution was an arranged marriage, and Snorri was married to a wealthy woman named Herdis. He eventually inherited her father's estate and chieftainship. But Snorri was a better poet than husband, and after having two children with Herdis, and several other children with several other women, he left his wife and moved to another estate.

In 1215, he was elected lawspeaker of the Althing, essentially the leader of the early centralized Icelandic government, and became well acquainted with King Hakon of Norway. Snorri spent some time in Norway with the king and other royals, primarily studying history. Seizing the opportunity, King Hakon

asked Snorri to swear an oath of loyalty, gave him a promotion, and asked him to serve as the spokesman for the King of Norway in Iceland. Politically speaking, Hakon was using Snorri to facilitate loyalty in Iceland so that he might incorporate Iceland into the Norwegian kingdom. Snorri was reelected as lawspeaker in 1222, due mostly to his name recognition as a great poet, but his controversial political agenda was to consolidate as much of Iceland as he could, forming alliances with other chieftains.

He remarried to a wealthy widow named Hallveig, who also happened to be the granddaughter of his foster father, Jon, so that when the time came, Snorri could deliver Iceland to King Hakon and receive great gratitude from the king. But the other chieftains soon caught on, which led to fighting and political instability in Iceland. Not quite as brave as the legendary heroes he wrote about, Snorri was not particularly successful on the battlefield, and not as savvy with strategies of war and politics as he could have been.

About that time, Norway was destabilizing, too, and Hakon's hold on the throne was challenged. Snorri started to express discontent and tried to remove himself from politics altogether. Realizing that Snorri's position had been compromised, and knowing Snorri could be erratic and fickle, Hakon refused to allow Snorri to leave Norway and return home to Iceland, claiming that he needed Snorri's loyal assistance but secretly fearing that Snorri would help his opponents. But Snorri disobeyed the king and snuck home anyway, and the king sent agents to Iceland after him, with orders that he be captured or killed. These agents may or may not have given him the option to be captured (still up for historical debate!), but they definitely did execute him as he ran to hide in his own cellar. (This cellar was accessible via a tunnel leading from his outdoor hot tub, and Snorri's hot tub is a preserved archaeological site that can still be visited in Iceland today!) It's recorded that his last words were a variation on the theme "Don't shoot!"

Despite the fact that many Norwegians and Icelanders deeply mourned the great author's murder, the Norwegian king's grand scheme of absorbing Iceland nonetheless succeeded. By 1262, the Icelandic Althing had been pressured into accepting Norwegian royal authority and swore allegiance to the king. But centuries after his death, Snorri's legacy lives on in his detailed and colorful renderings of the myths and legends of his own ancestors, to the gratitude and enjoyment of many.

FURTHER READING

In addition to the primary sources listed in Part 1, here are a few other resources to continue learning about Norse mythology, history, literature, and language.

BOOKS

Look for the newest versions of these titles:

Dictionary of Northern Mythology by Rudolf Simek (English translation by Angela Hall), published by D.S. Brewer. Reference guide (with citations) to Norse and other related medieval Germanic and Roman mythological places, names, objects, and common words.

Norse Mythology: A Guide to Gods, Heroes, Rituals, and Beliefs by John Lindow, published by Oxford University Press. Another reference guide comprising fewer but lengthier entries; includes scholastic commentary.

The Norse Myths: A Guide to the Gods and Heroes by Carolyne Larrington, published by Thames & Hudson. An introduction to the Norse myths presented in a more holistic, narrative form, rather than individual entries.

Norse Mythology by Neil Gaiman, published by W.W. Norton and Company. Gaiman retells a selection of Norse myths in the same evocative writing style as his other bestselling fiction books.

D'Aulaires' Book of Norse Myths by Ingri and Edgar Parin d'Aulaire, published by New York Review Children's Collection. For those who read with children, this is a classic family-friendly version: less traumatizing, but maintains the original stories with playful illustrations (ages 5–10).

The Viking Age: A Reader edited by Angus A. Somerville and R. Andrew McDonald, published by University of Toronto Press. English translations of primary sources about life in Viking-era Scandinavia, including but not limited to mythology.

A New Introduction to Old Norse by Michael Barnes and Anthony Faulkes, published by Viking Society for Northern Research. If you're up for a challenge and decide you want to learn the Old Norse language, these volumes will get you started!

PODCASTS AND OTHER CONTENT

The History of Vikings by Noah Tetzner (find it on Apple Podcasts). Noah Tetzner hosts informal conversations with scholars and specialists on various subjects relating to Viking history and Norse mythology.

Jackson Crawford's Old Norse Channel (search "Jackson Crawford" on *YouTube*). Crawford's growing library of more than two hundred videos featuring detailed but accessible discussions about Old Norse language and literature.

English–Old Norse Dictionary by Ross G. Arthur. A searchable PDF dictionary hosted by York University, to look through some interesting words: www.yorku.ca/inpar/language/English-Old _Norse.pdf.

Index

ABOUT THE AUTHOR

Kelsey A. Fuller-Shafer completed her PhD in ethnomusicology at the University of Colorado Boulder. Her doctoral research focused on contemporary popular music, gender studies, and political commentary of Sámi (the Indigenous people of northern Fenno-Scandinavia) artists and scholars. She has guest lectured at several universities and presented research at numerous conferences and symposia in both the United States and Sweden on subjects ranging from Swedish jazz to Sámi pop, and from Norse myth to Eurovision. Kelsey has broad teaching experience that includes courses in music, language, literature, folklore, and Nordic history at the University of Colorado Boulder and Augustana College. She has also worked as a library and archives assistant in the Swenson Swedish Immigration Research Center. Kelsey is currently serving as the supervisor of access services at the DiMenna-Nyselius Library at Fairfield University. Calling various parts of New England home, Kelsey is originally from Connecticut and earned her BA in music from Eastern Connecticut State University.

ABOUT THE ILLUSTRATOR

Sara Richard is an Eisner and Ringo Award–nominated artist from New Hampshire. She has worked in the comic book industry for a decade, mainly as a cover artist. Sara's inspiration comes from Art Deco, Art Nouveau, 1980s fashion, and Victorian-era design. When not making art or writing, she's watching horror movies, cleaning forgotten gravestones, and collecting possibly haunted curios from the nineteenth century. Her online gallery can be found at SaraRichard.com.

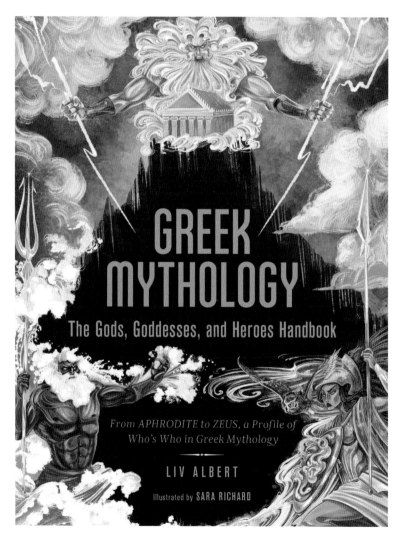